THE BLUE JEAN BOOK

THE BLUE JEAN BOOK

**The Story
Behind the Seams**

by Tanya Lloyd Kyi

ANNICK PRESS
TORONTO + NEW YORK + VANCOUVER

Text © 2005 Tanya Lloyd Kyi
Second Printing, February 2007

Annick Press Ltd.

We acknowledge the support of the Canada Council for the Arts, the Ontario Arts Council, and the Government of Canada through the Book Publishing Industry Development Program (BPIDP) for our publishing activities.

Edited by Pam Robertson
Copy edited by John Sweet
Photo research by John Sweet
Cover and interior design by Irvin Cheung & Peter Pimentel/iCheung Design
Front cover photos: iStock/Amanda Rohde; Courtesy Lee Jeans Archives; Courtesy Wrangler Jeans Archives. Special thanks to Maggie Woo
Back cover photo: Courtesy Levi Strauss & Co. Archives

The text was typeset in Celeste, Info, and GoldenGate.

Cataloging in Publication
Kyi, Tanya Lloyd, 1973–
The blue jean book : the story behind the seams / Tanya Lloyd Kyi.

Includes bibliographical references and index.
ISBN 1-55037-917-8 (bound).—ISBN 1-55037-916-X (pbk.)

1. Jeans (Clothing)—History. 2. Jeans (Clothing) I. Title.

GT2085.K95 2005   391
C2005-901434-2

Printed and bound in China

Published in the U.S.A. by:	**Distributed in Canada by:**	**Distributed in the U.S.A. by:**
Annick Press (U.S.) Ltd.	Firefly Books Ltd.	Firefly Books (U.S.) Inc.
	66 Leek Crescent	P.O. Box 1338
	Richmond Hill, ON	Ellicott Station
	L4B 1H1	Buffalo, NY 14205

Visit our website at: **www.annickpress.com**

CONTENTS

INTRODUCTION

Jeans—they're practically in our genes. People have been buying pairs ever since Levi Strauss made the first ones in California in 1873. And the love of denim has traveled from North America around the world. Teenagers in Europe, Asia, and South America are wearing some of the same brands as we are. Even in places where everything else seems different, jeans are still jeans. Ever notice that when the evening news shows a student protest in Pakistan or a peace rally in Israel, everyone's pants are the same? Jeans transcend nationality, race, and even war, yet they're one of the most ordinary parts of our lives.

Magic comes in many forms. Tonight it comes to us in a pair of pants. I hereby propose that these Pants belong to us equally, that they will travel to all the places we're going, and they will keep us together when we are apart.

— from *The Sisterhood of the Traveling Pants* by Ann Brashares

For some people, searching for the perfect jeans is like finding the ideal bathing suit. They spend days or weeks combing the malls for the pair that lengthens their legs or hugs their hips. Other people scour garage sales and flea markets looking for a well-worn pair, complete with uneven fading and rips in the knees.

Often we choose our jeans because of how they make us feel, as well as how they make us look. In *The Sisterhood of the Traveling Pants,* four friends stumble upon a pair of used jeans that somehow magically fits their different shapes and sizes. They decide to mail them back and forth during their first summer apart. As the jeans arrive in new parts of the world, they lend each girl the strength and confidence to face the confusing situations in her life.

We don't all expect magic, but there's no doubt that we love our favorite pairs. Why are we so attached to them? They're comfortable and they don't need to be ironed. You can eat a bag of chips, wipe your hands on your butt, and the grease doesn't show. You can lend them to a friend, wear them in the mud, let them mildew in the bottom of the laundry hamper for a few weeks and it makes no difference: as soon as they're washed, they're as good as new.

Pants with Pull

Jeans have always been famous for their strength. In 1938, Elton Schram of Belmont, California, used a pair as a tow rope! Elton wrote Levi Strauss & Co. a letter explaining how he had found a friend stranded in his car at the side of the road. He was ready to tow his friend the six kilometers (four miles) to the nearest town, but neither man had a rope. Then Elton remembered the old pair of Levi's he had in his trunk. He tied one pant leg to each car and successfully rescued his friend. The pants survived without a single tear.

In 1939, the Lee Company teamed up with Ripley's Believe It or Not! to create a series of advertisements celebrating the strength of Lee jeans. Cartoonist and writer Robert Ripley specialized in collecting amazing information. In one ad, Ripley used a 4.5-tonne

Jeans are controversial in some parts of the world. In Turkey, church and government leaders continue to argue about whether women and girls should dress traditionally, in skirts and scarves, or in Western-style outfits.

(5-ton) steamroller to iron a pair of Lee overalls. When they were peeled off the pavement, the pants were unharmed and the buttons had held their shape. In another test, one man stood in the pockets of another man's overalls, without tearing the stitching.

In 1999, scientists from Cornell University and the Sciencenter of Ithaca used seven pairs of blue jeans to lift a 1,600-kilogram (3,500-pound) station wagon into the air. When the jeans survived, the scientists lowered the car, removed one pair, and hoisted it again. The jeans still held. They continued removing one pair at a time until the car was dangling by a single pair. Spectators heard the threads begin to snap moments before the car tipped toward the ground. Finally, the jeans had given way, ripping just above the knees.

Blue Beginnings

Jeans are such a basic part of our everyday lives that we never stop to think about where they come from. In fact, our favorite pants are born as cream-colored puffs of cotton.

Grown in warm, dry climates, raw cotton is harvested and taken to a fac-

COTTON TALES

Have you eaten any cotton today? You may have—cotton fiber and seeds are used in many products, including margarine and vegetable oil. The plant is also used to make mops, soap, paper, and candles.

tory called a cotton gin, where pipes suck the cotton out of the trucks or train cars and into the building. There, huge dryers remove any excess moisture, then a machine combs through the fibers to screen out sticks and dirt. Finally, another machine called a gin stand plucks the cotton fibers away from the seeds. The clean fibers are shipped to spinning mills, where they are spun into stone-colored cloth— what we think of as plain cotton fabric.

In the 1890s, the first jeans makers ordered denim from the Amokseag Mill in Manchester, New Hampshire, and

(above) This photo from the Sciencenter in Ithaca, New York, shows how a crane lifted a station wagon off the ground using only blue jeans. The demonstration was part of an exhibit on the high-tech nature of our clothes, from jeans to bulletproof vests.

(opposite page) According to this 1939 Lee ad, jeans are almost indestructible. One man crawled the length of a marathon on his knees without wearing out the denim.

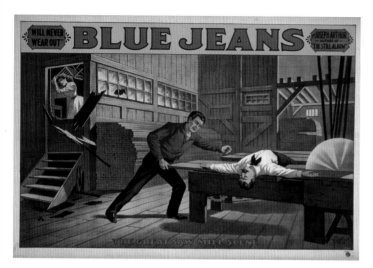

By the late 1800s, "jeans" was already a household term. This poster is for a play called *Blue Jeans*—a melodrama that appeared onstage in 1899.

of the most expensive dyes in the world. Then, in 1880, German chemist Johann von Baeyer discovered a way to create the same color in the laboratory. Soon a German chemical company was selling synthetic indigo for much lower prices than the plant-based dye.

Today, companies around the world produce more than 12,600 tonnes (14,000 tons) of synthetic indigo every year, and much of it is used to dye blue jeans. Like the original, naturally produced indigo, the synthetic dye isn't colorfast. That means it will slowly fade or wash out of fabric. Have a peek at your jeans. Are they still saturated in dye, or have they paled to a baby blue? Some people love it when their old jeans have become soft and faded, but others head for the mall to buy a new pair as soon as their denim loses its crisp dark color.

requested not pale beige but dark blue, a color that would show less dirt and wear. The mill received the orders and prepared to send shipments of their blue cotton denim, which they colored with indigo. Indigo was a dye made by fermenting the leaves of the indigo plant, which grew up to two meters (six feet) tall in the tropical climates of Africa and Southeast Asia.

Because the leaves had to be fermented, making indigo took a lot of time and labor. For centuries it was one

Factory Facts

Denim arrives at the jeans factory in enormous rolls of 450 meters (490 yards). Each roll provides enough fabric to make 300 pairs of jeans. An automated cutting machine slices through 68 layers of fabric at once, creating perfectly patterned cut-outs. Each cut piece is then passed to workers with sewing machines.

First, all the details such as pockets and belt loops are created. A giant

MARCO POLO LEAVES HIS MARK

Indigo was named by the explorer Marco Polo as he traveled across what is now Pakistan. He saw the plant being used to dye fabric in the Indus Valley.

When the American cotton industry was born, plantation owners depended on slave labor to keep prices down. In 1860, there were almost 4 million slaves in the southern United States, many forced to work from sunrise until sunset or face the overseer's whip.

HISTORY OF SEA ISLAND COTTON.—From Sketches by James E. Taylor.—SEE PAGE 75.

SORTING COTTON.

SEA ISLAND COTTON PLANT.

and cotton plantation, near the mouth of the Savannah river, presents a more vivid idea of work in the busy season of getting in the crop than mere language can convey.

In the "sorting" and "moting-room" we have the laborers busily employed in the foreground, in carefully assorting the different qualities of cotton, which work consists in separating the stained cotton from the purely white, and also putting together the staple which is most perfectly grown, leaving the blasted and unripe staple either to be rejected altogether, or to be sold as inferior quality. Against the rear walls of the room are to be seen the women engaged in "moting," which process consists of placing the staple in boxes —the bottoms of which are wire-sleeves.

By gently patting and pressing the staple, it is relieved of all dust and sand, and prepared for the next process, which consists of "whipping." Here the "locks" are entirely opened, and the cotton begins to assume the light and merchantable appearance, and is at last prepared for the important work of separating the staple from the seed.

If cotton from the field is weighed,

CARRYING COTTON FROM THE FIELD TO THE GIN.

PLANTING.

WEIGHING.

Workers at a Mexican factory unroll a bolt of denim. Many American workers lost their jobs in the 1980s when jeans factories moved to foreign countries with cheaper labor. Yet even workers in places like Mexico may soon be replaced by machines.

TURNING JEANS INTO COLD HARD CASH

Every year, truckloads of jeans and other cotton clothing are recycled and turned back into cotton fiber. This fiber is used to create strong, flexible paper—the type used in the printing of money. It's stronger than paper made from wood fiber, and better able to withstand the wear and tear that money goes through as it journeys from wallet to wallet.

stamp slams down onto a cookie-cutter-like mold, creating 20 pockets at a time, and another machine folds, sews, and presses each pocket in place. A zipper machine stitches the zipper to the denim, cuts it to size, and attaches the pull tab. Needles pull cotton thread through the fabric 4,000 times a minute.

When the pieces are assembled, workers stitch them together. The person responsible for stitching the in-seams works on more than 750 pairs of pants each day. At the end of the sewing line there are machines to steam press the pants and turn them right-side-out. From the first snip to the final steam, the entire pant-making process takes less than 10 minutes.

Why We're Blue

None of this explains why jeans are so popular. More than half a billion pairs are sold in North America each year, and people around the world are crazy about them. In 2001, one fashion designer even joined forces with a jeweler to create a pair of jeans studded with diamonds and rhinestones. The hip-huggers were modeled at the Gattinoni Couture fashion show in Milan, Italy, and sold for about US$500,000.

Obviously, we're not all going to cough up half a million dollars for a pair of pants. But we regularly pay $50 or $75, and most of us buy at least one new pair each year. Are jeans popular just because they're strong? Because they're what we've always worn? Or is it that the perfect pair of jeans makes us feel like we fit in, like we're as cool as every other jean-wearing kid on the block?

Researchers have suggested that we're actually happier wearing jeans. One study showed that when people were allowed to wear casual clothes like jeans to work, they called in sick less often. Scientists at the University of Wisconsin studied more than 50 workers who wore jeans to the office on Fridays. They took an average of 491 more steps wearing jeans than they did in their dress clothes, and burned an extra 25 calories a day. So not only did they put more energy into their jobs, but they worked off some flab, too.

But we don't need scientific data to tell us that we love our jeans. We've been wearing them since we were babies. Our parents wore them, and our grandparents wore them. In fact, North Americans have been wearing jeans for more than a century, thanks to a businessman, a tailor, and a gold rush. It all started with Levi Strauss on a ship bound for California…

PLENTIFUL PANTS

Levi Strauss & Co. is one of the world's largest clothing companies and has sold more than 3.5 billion pairs of jeans around the world. If you lined all these pants up lengthwise, they would stretch to the moon and back seven times.

CHAPTER 1

THE BIRTH OF THE BLUES

Pants with a Past

Levi Strauss joined the other passengers on deck as the ship steamed into San Francisco's harbor. He had been traveling for weeks, first journeying south from New York along the Eastern Seaboard, then across Panama, and finally on a steamer chugging north to California. Levi couldn't wait to step onto the docks of San Francisco.

It was 1853, and according to the newspaper reports in the East, this city's streets were paved with gold nuggets, and gold dust was so plentiful that it stuck to people's clothes. It's no wonder that the ship's passengers pushed along the gangway as soon as it was lowered. Elbowing his way through the crowds, 24-year-old Levi felt as if the earth were bucking and swaying beneath him. After the constant movement of the ship, his legs couldn't adjust to walking on solid ground.

The streets extending in front of him were paved not with gold but with cobblestones. Men in silk hats and long coats passed briskly on plank sidewalks. There were a few women, easy to spot in their hoop skirts. Street lamps filled with kerosene or whale oil rose above the bustle. Gazing about his new city, Levi sighed with satisfaction. He had finally arrived. Tomorrow he would begin his own quest for success.

Who the Heck was Loeb Strauss?

Levi Strauss was actually named Loeb when he was born in Buttenheim, Bavaria, in 1829. He was the youngest son in a large family. After his father died, Loeb immigrated to New York to join his two older brothers, who had started a business called J. Strauss Brother & Co. Soon after Loeb arrived and began working there, he started to call himself Levy. It's possible that this was a nickname given to him by his customers, but it's more likely that he chose it himself, wanting a name that

was easier for his American clientele to pronounce and remember. He applied for American citizenship in 1847, gave his name as Levy in the 1850 census, and began spelling it "Levi" shortly after.

By the time Levi opened his San Francisco wholesale business, he had years of experience selling goods for his brothers. The weeks he had spent on

He may not look like the coolest guy, but those sideburns were actually stylish in the 1860s. Levi Strauss made the best business decision of his life when he helped Jacob Davis patent and sell the first pairs of jeans.

This building on San Francisco's Battery Street served as the headquarters of Levi Strauss & Co. from 1866 until 1906, when an earthquake destroyed much of the city.

Most of what he stocked was considered "dry goods": clothing, fabric, blankets, needles, thread, scissors, canvas, handkerchiefs, pillows, and underwear. Levi sold these supplies to small stores throughout California.

Heavy-duty work pants were one of the most popular items sold through Levi's wholesale business. Many of the hopeful prospectors were city slickers who had arrived in city clothing. (Just imagine a group of New York stockbrokers setting off on a camping trip in their dress suits!) As they scrambled up and down the banks of the American River, they soon tore holes in the bottoms and ripped the knees of their pants.

Levi's work pants and his other products sold so well that in 1866 he moved his business to a larger location on busy Battery Street. To celebrate the company's success, he outfitted the new building with the leading technologies of the time: elevators and gas chandeliers.

By the time the California gold rush drew to a close in the mid-1860s, Levi was well on his way to making his fortune, one of the few who actually did strike it rich.

board the ship to California, learning about gold miners, were an added bonus.

Shovels, gold pans, scales, buckets, boots, frying pans, eating utensils, and even rifles—prospectors arrived in California with goods of every description piled into their packs. Many of the miners were young men with gold fever glinting in their eyes. All they could think about was the precious metal waiting beneath the next inch of soil or in the next scoop of sand from the river.

Levi also had a touch of gold fever. But he hadn't traveled to California to find his fortune in the goldfields—he intended to get rich selling supplies.

A Riveting Idea

When their gold pans came up empty in California, Americans looked for riches elsewhere. In the early 1870s, silver turned up in Nevada, lying in thick seams in the ground, and prospectors rushed there. Soon boom towns were springing up and lucky miners were bragging of bigger and bigger bonanzas.

Inside a tailor's shop in the mining town of Reno, Nevada, Jacob Davis stopped to rub his temples and gaze at the ragged pair of work pants on the table in front of him. How could he make his work pants stronger? Just that morning he'd met with a woman who wanted better pants that her husband could wear while chopping wood. And the miners were constantly stuffing too much rock in their pockets and ripping the seams.

Jacob had done everything he could to make the denim work pants tough, including ordering high-quality fabric directly from Levi Strauss in San Francisco. But men still managed to rip the pockets. If Jacob didn't find a solution quickly, he was going to lose his reputation as a skilled tailor.

Like Levi Strauss, Jacob was an immigrant. He was born in Latvia, to the west of Russia. And just as Levi had done 20 years before, Jacob was trying to build his own bonanza by selling clothing and equipment to miners. He only needed to create pants that wouldn't tear.

As Jacob fretted about the dilemma, he gazed out at the busy street. A few men chatted in groups on the corners, some carried bags of supplies down the sidewalks, others hitched their horses to the nearby posts.

Suddenly his eyes landed on the reinforced seam of a horse blanket. That was it! The strong copper rivets used in riding equipment and leather work could be used on pants as well. Soon, Jacob had a new pair of pants made. He began pounding metal rivets into the corners of each pocket and at the bottom of the button fly. Finally he had found a way to make his work pants stronger—strong enough even for miners!

Selling Like Hot Pants

Jacob's new riveted pants were so tough that prospectors bought pairs as quickly as Jacob could produce them. Now Jacob was raking in cash, but he had one big worry: what if someone stole his idea? Another tailor could make his own riveted pants, sell them for less, and Jacob's profits would disappear.

Just as miners claimed their silver strikes, Jacob decided to stake a claim on his riveted pants. He wrote to the U.S. Patent and Trademark Office. Then he ran into a problem—a $68 problem. That was the fee the government charged to issue a patent. It was about the price of a parlor piano, or about half the cost of a ship voyage to London. It was certainly more money than Jacob had to invest.

He turned to his main supplier, Levi Strauss, for help. In a

The oldest pair of 501 jeans still in existence, these pants date from about 1879. Though we no longer need suspender clips on our waistbands, our styles today aren't that different.

letter to San Francisco, Jacob proposed that Levi join him in a partnership, sharing the production costs and the profits from the new style.

At the head offices of the modern-day Levi Strauss & Co. in San Francisco, there is a letter typed on carbon paper and titled "Transcription." The letter reads in part:

> *The secratt of them pants is the Rivits that I put in those pockets and I found demand so large that I cannot make them up fast enough. I knew you can make a very large amount of money on it if you make up pants the way I do.*

Is this the original letter from Jacob Davis to Levi Strauss? We can't be sure. It might be, or it might be a piece of creative writing, the work of someone trying to re-create Jacob's story.

Either way, Jacob Davis did manage to convince Levi Strauss to invest. Together the two men applied for a patent, and on May 20, 1873, the U.S. Patent and Trademark Office issued patent number 139,121, protecting the invention of riveted pants.

Blue jeans were born! They still weren't called jeans, though. They were known as waist-high overalls, or waist overalls. They were a bit baggy, there was only one back pocket, and instead of belt loops the pants had suspender buttons. They had a button fly, and a buckle at the back of the waistline allowed men to cinch them up. But despite these differences, the pants looked a lot like our blue jeans today. If a guy in your homeroom wore the 1873 style, the crotch would be loose, the legs baggy, and, without suspenders, the waistband of his underwear would show. You might think he was wearing a hot new retro look.

Here's how one newspaper, the *Pacific Rural Press*, welcomed riveted pants in 1873:

> *Simple as this device seems, nevertheless it is quite effective, and we do not doubt that his manufacture, of overalls especially, will become quite popular amongst our working men, as the overalls are made and cut in the style of the best custom made pants. Nothing looks more slouchy in a workman than to see his pockets ripped open and hanging down, and no other part of the clothing is so apt to be torn and ripped as the pockets. Besides its slouchy appearance, it is inconvenient and often results in the person losing things from his pockets.*

Within a short time the new riveted pants were wildly successful. Levi invited Jacob to move to San Francisco

Levi Strauss & Co. gave this advertisement to store owners in the late 1890s. In the middle of the ad you can see the Two-Horse brand logo—a pair of work-horses trying to rip apart a pair of Levi's.

and supervise the manufacturing of the waist overalls. Jacob supervised those who cut the fabric, then sent the cut pieces to seamstresses, who worked from their homes, sewing the pants by hand. The rivets were also applied by hand; workers used a maul to pound them into the fabric. Soon the seamstresses couldn't keep up with demand. Instead of paying people to sew in their homes, Levi and Jacob hired dozens of seamstresses and opened new factories. Business was booming!

The Lowdown on Denim

American factories began producing denim from cotton in the late 1700s. But the name "denim" came from a French fabric woven of silk and wool. Because the fabric was made in Nimes, France, it was called "serge de Nimes." When stores in England began importing the cloth, its name was eventually shortened to "deNimes" or "denim." Denim was one of the world's strongest fabrics at the time. In fact, some histo-

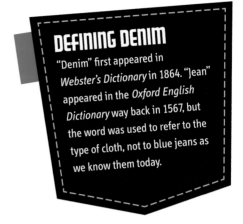

DEFINING DENIM
"Denim" first appeared in *Webster's Dictionary* in 1864. "Jean" appeared in the *Oxford English Dictionary* way back in 1567, but the word was used to refer to the type of cloth, not to blue jeans as we know them today.

rians believe that the ships taken to the New World by Christopher Columbus had denim sails.

The first cloth called "jean" was made in Genoa, Italy, and was worn by sailors. In Italian, "Genoa" is pronounced "Genes." Levi Strauss didn't use Italian fabric, and his denim cloth wasn't the same as that worn by sailors, so he never liked the word "jeans." To him, it was just plain wrong. It wasn't until years after his death that Levi Strauss & Co. began using the word.

Getting the Market All Stitched Up

Each pair of Levi's had curved orange stitching on the back pocket, called the Arcuate design. The curves looked almost like the outstretched wings of a bird.

Between 1890 and 1943, other companies saw how well Levi Strauss & Co. was doing and began making their own dark denim pants with wing-shaped back-pocket patterns. To stop the imitators Levi Strauss & Co. registered the Arcuate design as a trademark in 1943.

As Levi's waist overalls became

This pair of 501 jeans from 1933 displays the Arcuate design—the double orange wings— on the back pocket. The same design appears on Levi's jeans today.

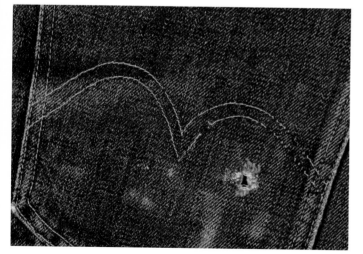

more and more popular, the company assigned numbers to their different styles. The original design from 1873 was given the number 501, and 501 jeans were born. (Why the number 501? Nobody really knows—the records were lost in the 1906 San Francisco earthquake.)

Levi Strauss wanted to tell the whole country how strong his pants were, but not everyone could read the company's newspaper advertisements; some of his customers were illiterate. Levi also wanted to create an image that people would associate with his jeans. So he had a leather label designed for the back waistband, showing a pair of jeans tied between two draft horses. Straining in opposite directions, the horses were trying to rip the pants apart, but the jeans were too tough to tear. The label worked so well that for years afterwards Levi's jeans were known as the Two-Horse brand.

Bargain Bottoms

In 1890, Levi's waist overalls cost about US$1 a pair. That was the equivalent of about US$20 today—enough to make Levi Strauss rich. By the time he died in 1902 at age 73, he had saved a fortune and donated a great deal of money to several community charities. His nephews Jacob, Sigmund, Abraham, and Louis Stern inherited Levi Strauss & Co. They were eager to build on the company's success, but they were facing a new challenge—competition.

SEEING THE SHRINK

When you buy jeans today, the fabric has been pre-shrunk. You can take them home and wash them and they'll remain almost the same length and width. But when the first jeans were sold, the fabric wasn't so sophisticated. Most waist overalls were large and baggy, designed for strength, not fashion. Still, there was one way you could shrink the fabric to fit: jump into a horse trough. The water shrunk the fabric, and if a man wore the jeans as they dried, they would mold to his individual shape. (Washing the jeans and wearing them wet would probably have done the same thing. Maybe gold miners thought that jumping in a horse trough was more fun than doing laundry.) The first pre-shrunk jeans weren't introduced until the early 1960s.

CHAPTER 2

MOVERS AND SHAKERS AND BLUE JEAN MAKERS

Henry David Lee's chauffeur sighed in frustration as he scuffed his way out from under Lee's automobile. There always seemed to be more things to fix, and every trip under the car meant more dirt and grease on his uniform, which meant more time cleaning his clothes. He was a chauffeur, not a washing machine! There had to be a better way…

New Kid on the Block

The patent on riveted pants expired in 1891, allowing other companies to make their own versions of jeans. But Levi Strauss & Co. didn't face any major competition until the early 1900s, when clothing manufacturer Henry David Lee arrived on the scene.

Lee was born in Vermont in 1849 and began working in the oil industry as a young man. Then he began coughing. His chest hurt, he found it hard to breathe, and he woke up in the middle of the night sweating and shivering. The diagnosis: tuberculosis. His doctor told him to move to the cleaner air of the American West. In 1889, Lee coughed his way to Salina, Kansas, and opened the H.D. Lee Mercantile Company, the largest food supplier between Kansas City and Denver. Once he recovered his health and his business took off, Lee began selling fabric, furniture, and stationery. Despite a massive warehouse fire and constant transportation difficulties—there were no paved highways in the early 1900s—the H.D. Lee Mercantile Company soon had customers all over the West.

Henry David Lee wasn't a patient man. So when his suppliers in the eastern United States couldn't guarantee him a reliable supply of work clothes, Lee opened his own factory and began making jackets and dungarees—pocketed pants with a flap over the chest and straps over the shoulders, similar to what we think of today as overalls. Soon after Lee began producing the clothing, his chauffeur started complaining about his clothes getting dirty when he worked under the car. One of the men—either Lee or his chauffeur—came up with the idea of stitching together a pair of pants and a long-sleeved shirt to form a denim coverall. The Lee Union-All (a union of dungarees and long-sleeved work shirts) was born. It was first marketed to men who loved cars:

On or Off in a Jiffy—and as comfortable as an old shoe, LEE UNION-ALLS are indispensable to motoring. For men who own pleasure cars their usefulness is manifest and a suit should be carried under a seat to protect

When Henry David Lee moved to Kansas to start his mercantile business, his lawyer thought he was crazy. He said, "I've stood beside you, Mr. Lee, in many battles… Now if you persist in going out west, it looks like there remains only one service I can render you: that is to bring your body back for an Ohio burial."

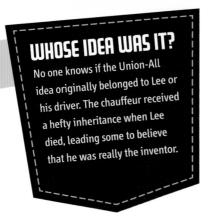

This 1919 advertisement for women's Union-Alls argued that skirts weren't practical for workers as they could get caught in the machinery of a modern factory. (High heels, apparently, were still okay.)

clothing when tire trouble occurs. Drivers of trucks and motor mechanics, having once ascertained the good sense, economical features of LEE UNION-ALLS never wear anything else during working hours.

— Lee advertisement, 1913

The khaki-colored Union-All wasn't going to win any fashion awards. It looked like the coveralls worn by today's mechanics: a heavy-duty jumpsuit with long sleeves to protect the wearer from dirt and scratches. Each pair had two back pockets, two hip pockets, and two button-up pockets on the chest—perfect for carrying an assortment of tools. There were a few touches of style—wide collars, tailored cuffs at the wrists, and rolled cuffs at the ankles—but the Union-All was all about hard work. In 1913, it was an instant success with farmers, engineers, and factory workers, and Lee had to open three factories to keep up with the demand. Within a year, Union-Alls were also available for women and children.

THE 1910s: JEANS WERE THERE

As H.D. Lee was producing his first Union-Alls, other inventions were changing the world around him. Henry Ford and the Ford Motor Company introduced the first Model T in 1908. General Motors began producing Frigidaire refrigerators for home use, replacing iceboxes. German physicist Wilhelm Roentgen discovered X-rays, and Marie Curie discovered radium, becoming the first woman to win a Nobel Prize.

There was a darker side to the decade: World War I began in 1914. As the American army prepared in 1917 to join the battles raging in Europe, Brigadier General Leonard Wood found that Lee Union-Alls were more durable than any other clothing. He ordered thousands for American soldiers, asking the company to supply as many pairs as they could manufacture. Ads from that time show American soldiers dressed in exactly the same style of Union-All worn by workers.

HOT-IRON BRANDED
HAIR-ON-HIDE LABEL

Lee
COWBOY PANTS

THE ONLY COWBOY PANT WITH ALL THESE FEATURES: Sanforized 11½-ounce Cowboy Denim; V-Shaped Saddle Crotch; Scratch-Proof Hip Pocket Rivets; Hot-Iron Branded Hair-on-Hide Label; Good Fit; Good Looks. Guaranteed. Sold by most good dealers.

Home on the Range

If you were looking for nightlife in the 1920s, you wouldn't head to the American West. There were way more cows than people. Thousands of cattle roamed sprawling ranchlands, and the men responsible for rounding up these herds and driving them to market were strong, silent types. (A good thing, since they only had cows to talk to.) According to the cowboy rep, they were tough, hard-working, loyal—and quick with their guns.

To the bigwigs of Hollywood, cowboys were ideal heroes. Soon movies about the Wild West were playing in theaters across the country. Stern men dressed in wide-brimmed hats, handkerchiefs, leather vests, boots, spurs, and of course jeans strutted their way onto the big screen. They rescued damsels, battled Indians, and cut the reins of runaway stagecoaches.

For both real cowboys and their Hollywood counterparts, the Lee Company introduced the 101 Cowboy Pant in 1924. It boasted thicker denim that could stand up to hours of friction against a saddle, rivets placed where they wouldn't scratch the saddle's leather, and a U-shaped crotch that gave men a little more room, making them more comfortable while riding.

Lee Cowboy Pants were invented by an exotic dancer, Sally Rand. Sally and her husband, rodeo star Turk Greenough, were invited to a Lee Company meeting to demonstrate how Sally took apart regular jeans and remade them into a tighter style.

Just Chillin'

Imagine you're an Iowa farmer, inspecting your fences at the end of December. It's bitterly cold, an icy wind is pushing you along, and your teeth are chattering. The only thing saving your fingers is a heavy pair of leather gloves.

Then you run into a problem. You have to pee. And in order to pee, you have to undo the button fly of your Lee Cowboy Pants. You have to take off your gloves and fumble the buttons open with cold-stiffened fingers. Now your hands—along with certain other parts—are freezing!

In response to farmers' concerns, the Lee Company revolutionized jeans in 1926. They replaced the button fly with a new invention… the zipper. They called it the "hookless fastener." While hookless fasteners had already been used for several years on shoes and tobacco pouches, the Lee Company was the first to add them to men's jeans. To help promote the new style, the company held a contest to name zippered pants. The winning entry was "Whizit," after the sound made by the new zippers.

SALES AT SEA

Ahoy there, mate! Where did you buy those swashbuckling jeans? When their 101 Cowboy Pant proved successful, Lee also introduced pairs designed specifically for sailors and loggers.

Jeans changed forever when Lee introduced the zipper or "hookless fastener" in 1926. The company held a contest to name a line of overalls and play suits featuring the innovation, and the winning entry was "Whizit."

Presto… It's Open! Presto… It's Closed! Quick as a flash you can open or close the new Lee Buttonless Union-Alls, Overalls and Play Suits. Quick as a flash the whole family recognizes the comfort and convenience of these remarkable new work and play garments. The Hookless Fastener will not jam, rust or break and launders with perfect safety.

— Lee advertisement, 1927

Levi Strauss & Co. was also coming up with new ideas. To keep up with changes in men's fashion, belt loops gradually replaced the suspender buttons on most jeans (although for several years snap-on buttons allowed men to wear suspenders if they chose).

Denim in the Dirty Thirties

In the Roaring Twenties, people celebrated progress and believed that if they worked hard, they could live well. Then, in 1929, stock markets around the world crashed. People lost their savings, businesses and banks closed, and the American economy was plunged into a dark decade now known as the Great Depression or the Dirty Thirties. In 1933, more than 15 million Americans were without work; the unemployment rate stood at 25 percent.

Farmers in the 1930s found their crops worth little and their farms in danger of bankruptcy. To make matters worse, a drought swept across the Plains and left once-fertile fields looking more like dust bowls. Now that they couldn't afford to buy new clothes each season, farmers needed their long-lasting Levi's or Lee's more than ever. Photos of the era show entire families dressed in well-worn jeans.

The 1930s also threatened the cattle ranchers of the American West. The dry land could no longer support massive herds, and the animals couldn't be sold for the high profits of the past. Some creative ranchers found a new source of income—tourists. Capitalizing on the popularity of westerns, ranchers invited rich Americans from the East to experience the Wild West. The vacationers met real ranch hands, learned to ride the range, and copied the rugged look of the cowboys.

Have you ever seen an old John Wayne movie from the 1930s? An up-and-coming star, Wayne appeared onscreen dressed in boots, spurs, blue jeans, wide silver belt buckle, leather vest, handkerchief, and cowboy hat. Soon that was the look everyone wanted! Tourists returning home to New York or Chicago tried to look as rugged and tough as cowboys by wearing heeled boots and denim cowboy pants. Western clothes were even featured on the pages of the fashion magazine *Vogue.*

Despite the Depression, the Lee Company managed to convince people that jeans would last twice as long as other pants, making them a good investment. The company even opened a new factory in 1936, and celebrated its 50th anniversary in 1939 (an event it dubbed the Golden Jubi-Lee).

Levi Strauss & Co. was a larger company with more staff to pay and more factories to run. It struggled with lower sales but survived the decade with a few dashes of innovation. One of the company's main problems was competition; other jeans makers were producing dark blue denim pants with the Levi's Arcuate design on the back pocket. (The orange stitching had not yet been trademarked.) Levi's were still known for quality, but buyers had to be able to tell the real thing from cheaper copies. In 1936, the company's marketing wizards designed a small red tab for the back pocket of waist overalls, with the word *Levi's* stitched in white letters.

Today we're so used to seeing the red tab that we don't think twice about it. But in the 1930s, putting a tag on the *outside* of clothing was a new phenomenon. The flash of red drew people's eyes. Suddenly it was easy to identify a pair of Levi's from the other side of the street or from across a room. People wearing Levi's were basically carrying

Wrangler was the first jeans company to use a series of celebrities in their advertisements. Having a rodeo star endorse jeans in the 1940s would be like having a professional baseball or hockey player endorse them today.

RISING TO THE CHALLENGE

The "rise" of a pair of pants or overalls is the distance between the crotch and the waistline. Originally, overalls were available with different leg lengths, but they all had the same rise. On a short man the waistline might reach his ribs; a tall man could find the waistline of his overalls riding on his hips. In the 1930s, someone at Wrangler Jeans had the startling idea of adjusting the length of the rise to correspond with the length of the pant legs. The overalls were instantly more comfortable and sales boomed. Only one question remained: why had it taken 30 years to think of something so simple?

a mini-advertisement for the company on their back pocket. Since then, almost every clothing company has copied the idea. We wear shirts with brand names emblazoned across the chest, shoes with logos on the sides, and sunglasses with company names embossed on the plastic. Practically every time we leave the house, we become walking, talking billboards for clothing brands. And it all started with Levi's.

Lassoing Sales

Ride 'em, cowboys! In the 1940s there were only two big names in the world of jeans: Levi's and Lee. When Wrangler tried to enter the market, the company needed some way to convince buyers that it was a better brand. To do so, it used one of the most famous Wild West events: the rodeo. If the Wrangler logo decorated the backsides of bull-riding, calf-tying, lasso-throwing rodeo cowboys, who wouldn't want a pair?

Rodeos began as contests between working cowboys at the end of the 19th century in the American Southwest. These hardened horseback riders showed such skill that the events soon became spectator sports. It seemed as if each year brought tougher competitors, able to career around a course at breakneck speed and willing to risk their lives on bucking broncos. The men who won these competitions became instant heroes. Fans tried to act like them, talk like them, and dress like them.

Wrangler hired a Philadelphia tailor named Rodeo Ben to help design and market new cowboy pants. Already well known by the rodeo riders, Rodeo Ben had designed clothing for some of the most famous cowboys in the business. Soon champions such as Jim Shoulders, Bill Linderman, and Freckles Brown were wearing Wranglers. And since men across the West were copying the cowboys' strides and women were admiring the cowboys' butts, the jeans got a lot of attention! Wranglers proved so popular in Texas that the company opened a new factory in El Paso to meet the demand. In fact, so many riders across the country started wearing Wranglers that the Professional Rodeo Cowboys Association endorsed the jeans in 1947.

Cowboys were already popular Hollywood heroes. Now their characters became not only tough but sexy— even romantic. Among the Wild West heroes who sang their way onto the silver screen was Gene Autry. After he was "discovered" singing while working as a telegraph operator, he made dozens of western movies. In the midst of his gun-slinging, villain-chasing action scenes, Autry would pause to strum his guitar and break into a cowboy song.

Roy Rogers and his horse Trigger followed Autry onto the big screen. Hopalong Cassidy—actually actor William Boyd—did the same, starring in 66 feature films, 52 television shows, and more than 100 radio broadcasts. And nothing made him appear more like a cowboy than his well-worn, snug-fitting jeans.

Together, the three Wild West heroes won thousands of fans. Women swooned over the "singing cowboys," men flocked to the movies, and little boys across North America begged their parents for cowboy outfits. Autry, Rogers, and Cassidy each celebrated this success by releasing his own line of blue jeans.

Denim was definitely at home on the range. But in the cities, people still saw jeans as work clothes. Occasionally children might wear them for play, but no adult would ever wear them to the office or out to dinner. Women wouldn't wear them at all. And even though vacationers to the West might take home pairs of jeans as souvenirs, the market for the pants was still mainly limited to cowboys, farmers, and laborers. The real era of blue jeans was yet to come.

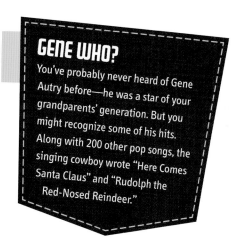

GENE WHO?

You've probably never heard of Gene Autry before—he was a star of your grandparents' generation. But you might recognize some of his hits. Along with 200 other pop songs, the singing cowboy wrote "Here Comes Santa Claus" and "Rudolph the Red-Nosed Reindeer."

CHAPTER 3

BLUE JEAN TIME MACHINE

How Denim Went Delinquent

From 1939 to 1945, the world went to war. The U.S. Army needed durable clothing for battle, and American blue jeans companies were there to provide it. This time the clothes they made for soldiers didn't look like blue jeans, but they shared the same thick fabric and strength. Blue Bell (the company that owned Wrangler Jeans) made 24 million items of military clothing during the war. Divided equally, that would mean each American soldier received two pieces of Blue Bell apparel. Lee also contributed, manufacturing combat suits, flight suits, and jackets.

At home in North America, wartime rationing led to shortages of blue jeans. To preserve fabric and thread for the war effort, Levi's dropped any extra details, including the flaps on the pockets of their jean jackets. The Arcuate design on the back pockets wasn't absolutely necessary either, so they dropped the stitching. However, rather than lose entirely the curves that they'd made so much effort to protect, the company had the design hand-painted on every pair. Still, fabric was so scarce that blue jeans were difficult to find in stores. At the bottom of an advertisement in *Life* magazine, Lee told its customers:

> *War conditions make it impossible to meet the growing demand for Lee Work Clothes. Your Lee Dealer is receiving his fair share of all we are able to make after the needs of our men in the armed forces have been supplied. If your Dealer is out of the Lee you want, please ask him to reserve one for you out of his next shipment.*

The shortage seemed to make jeans even more valued and popular; wearing the hard-to-find pants became a status symbol. Sometimes when a new shipment arrived, mobs of people would crowd into a store to snatch up pairs while they could.

American soldiers who were lucky enough to have blue jeans often carried their favorite pairs with them to training camps and overseas. In 1944, Levi Strauss & Co. received a letter from Mrs. I.B. MacKinnon, whose son was in the armed forces.

> *As soon as he left here and was sent to Hawaii for further training, my son wrote and asked us to send him three pair of Levis. Needless to say, we practically scoured the entire of San Francisco before we were able to get them for him. We mailed them to him*

WORLD WAR II: JEANS WERE THERE

In the first few decades of the 20th century, jeans were only available in North America. The companies had not yet expanded to other continents. When the United States joined World War II in 1941 and American soldiers set sail for Europe and Asia, they began to introduce blue jeans to the rest of the world.

> *and he thanked us profusely for them, and also said in the same letter that he was the envy of all the other boys in his detachment, and used to sleep with all three pair under him at night!*

The young soldier also told his mom that his Levi's fit better than the pants of his uniform. If he was forced to abandon ship on his way to the war overseas, he figured he would be able to swim faster in the tighter-fitting jeans.

Some men managed to keep their jeans with them through the entire war. As the fighting drew to a close, soldiers motorcycled through the German or Italian countryside wearing Levi's, or sampled the nightlife of Paris or London in their Wranglers. The people of Europe, having suffered through years of food and clothing shortages, were celebrating their freedom. The North American soldiers who had fought in the war were treated like heroes, and everything about them became popular—including their blue jeans.

For Men of Action!

POST

New SATURDAY EVENING **HINGE-BACK**

MARCH 41

Lee UNION-ALLS!

LEE TAILORED SIZES

A Perfect Fit For Every Build

Exclusive Treg Twills In Tailored Sizes Give More Comfort, Save You Money

Here it is! America's smart-looking, genuine Union-All in tailored sizes gives you more comfort, better looks and longer wear—or your money back! Lee's famous "Hinge-Back" automatically adjusts itself to give you new work

The Lee Union-Alls made for soldiers were also marketed to "men of action" on the home front.

Rosie the Riveter

As men rushed to join the war effort, there was no one left to run the assembly lines. Countries such as Britain and the United States were in desperate need of uniforms, armor, and weaponry, and they couldn't find workers to make them. Women came to the rescue. Some had been mothers or homemakers before the war began. Others had worked at low-paying jobs as seamstresses, secretaries, or teachers. Now they began wielding heavy machinery and learning trades.

In Britain during the 1930s, women were expected to stay at home. Those who did have jobs often quit when they got married. When the war began, the entire society changed. Everyone registered with the government, and 90 percent of single women and 80 percent of married women were asked to work for the war effort. One-third of the workers at chemical companies, metal industries, ship-building plants, and automakers were female.

Thousands of women also joined the workforce in Canada. When Queen Elizabeth toured the country in 1939, CBC Radio broadcast her personal message to Canadian women: "We, no less than men, have real and vital work to do for our country in its hour of need."

In North America a character named Rosie the Riveter became a symbol for working women, and she soon became a household name. In 1943, the *Saturday Evening Post* published a cover story about women joining the workforce, and famous artist Norman Rockwell painted a portrait of a working woman—"Rosie"—holding her power equipment.

What does all of this have to do with jeans? Well, the long skirts worn by women before the war were hardly practical for the assembly line. When Norman Rockwell drew his portrait, he put Rosie in safety goggles, rolled-up sleeves, and… denim coveralls. Partly because of the portrait, slacks or coveralls and bandanas became the patriotic dress code for North American women. In an American poster encouraging people to help the war effort, Rosie wore a denim jacket and a polka-dot bandana, showed her biceps, and proclaimed, "We Can Do It!"

When the war ended, governments and the returning soldiers expected women to leave their jobs and return to the home. Many did. But they didn't return to their Victorian-style skirts and blouses. Women had become accustomed to their new abilities and freedoms, including the right to wear blue jeans.

Levi's had created the first jeans designed specifically for women in 1935, and other companies soon followed. The Blue Bell Company called their new pants Jeanies. Advertisements announced, "Jeanies for Girls. The Perfect Garments for Work and Play." Similar ads from Lee promised, "Yessiree, These Lee Frontier Lady Pants are Tailored, Tapered, and Trim!" And it was Rodeo Ben, the celebrity designer hired

Rosie the Riveter encouraged women to roll up their sleeves and help with the war effort during World War II. In the United States, more than 6 million women joined the workforce. Though many lost their jobs when the soldiers returned home, they didn't forget the money they'd earned, the freedom they'd experienced, or the pants they'd worn.

by Wrangler, who first created jeans for women with a front zipper in the late 1940s. It seems strange now, but the new style wasn't popular—customers preferred the side zipper. It wasn't until the 1950s that the front zipper on women's pants caught on.

THE COLOR-BLIND BLUES

In the 1940s there was still a lot of racism in the United States, and African-American and white men usually worked in separate factories or even at separate companies. But when labor shortages during World War II threatened production, Levi Strauss & Co. hired African-American workers. For the first time, black and white workers did the same jobs at the same factories, as in this photo, taken at the Vallejo, California, factory of Levi Strauss & Co. It wasn't until 20 years later that the government passed laws forcing companies to let African-Americans work side by side with white employees.

Revving It Up!

When World War II ended, young soldiers were thrilled to return home, and some built their own motorcycles and went on joyrides around the country—the first teen rebels. They were no longer interested in the coveralls worn by their fathers and grandfathers. They wanted pants that fit snugly around the waist, suited more to motorcycle riding than to farming. Denim companies rushed to meet the demand. By 1947, Wrangler's advertising slogan had changed from "The World's Largest Producer of Work Clothes" to "The World's Largest Producer of Work and Play Clothes."

Just as cowboys had helped give jeans their tough, rugged appeal in the 1930s and 1940s, movie stars now gave jeans glamour. In 1953, Marlon Brando starred in a film called *The Wild One.* As the leader of the Black Rebels motorcycle gang, Brando was a slick, dark figure in a leather jacket, white T-shirt, and jeans. When a girl asked, "What are you rebelling against?" the tough hipster replied, "What da yah got?"

Women's jeans made their debut in the late 1930s. Soon, Lady Levi's, Lady Lee Riders, and Jeanies were competing for the market.

PRETTY IN PINK

When jeans companies introduced styles for women, they made small design changes to make the pants more feminine. One company sewed the selvage seams—where the fabric was stitched so it wouldn't fray—in pink thread instead of red.

Bad-boy movie star James Dean appeared in his signature style in *Giant*, the last movie he made before his death. A pair of Lee jeans worn by the actor are on display at the James Dean Memorial Gallery in Fairmount, Indiana.

knife fighting his enemies and playing "chickie" as he raced his car toward a cliff only to swerve at the last possible moment. Like Brando, Dean played it cool in white T-shirts and jeans.

In real life too, James Dean loved speed. As his career caught fire, he bought a racehorse, a motorcycle, and a Porsche sports car. Shortly before the premiere of *Rebel Without a Cause*, Dean crashed his Porsche and died instantly—a tragic death, but one that cemented his reputation as the ultimate bad boy.

While young men had Marlon Brando and James Dean to look up to, women had Marilyn Monroe. The blonde bombshell became the ultimate sex symbol of the 1950s after starring in movies such as *Gentlemen Prefer Blondes* and *How to Marry a Millionaire*. When she began wearing blue jeans that hugged her hips and showed off her curves at parties and in publicity photos, jeans became sexy for women, not just men.

To young people, jeans had once been the pants their dads wore to work; they were tough, but they were also worn and baggy. Movie stars such as Marlon Brando, James Dean, and Marilyn Monroe transformed the image of denim. It wasn't just for factory workers any more. Now jeans were something you might wear while you hung out with friends on Saturday night. You might even wear them on a date.

The Wild One celebrated teenage rebellion and violence—so much violence that it was banned in Britain until 1968. It sparked a trend toward rebel heroes, and James Dean was the next perfect candidate. With his dark hair, good looks, and intense eyes, he was an immediate teen idol. In his second film, *Rebel Without a Cause*, Dean played a "bad boy from a good family,"

Denim Goes Delinquent

As James Dean, Elvis Presley, and Marilyn Monroe attained superstar status, parents began worrying that young people were running wild. Were their sweet, innocent daughters being corrupted by television and movies? Could boys in tight pants and fast cars really be trusted? To parents who had lived through a depression and a war, these fun-loving young people seemed out of control. (One look at today's underwear- and cleavage-baring styles and the dads of the 1950s would have gone into cardiac arrest.)

In the 1950s movie *Blue Denim*, the blue-jean-wearing main character was a teenage girl, unmarried and pregnant. There were also motorcycle-riding, denim-wearing gang members. Were teenagers who wore jeans turning into juvenile delinquents? After decades of thinking of jeans as work clothes, suitable for the fields or the factory, parents had trouble adjusting to the idea of teens wearing jeans in high school hallways.

MARILYN AND ROSIE

When Rosie the Riveter encouraged women to join the workforce during World War II, the young Marilyn Monroe (then known as Norma Jean) responded. She worked at the Radio Plane Munitions Factory in Burbank, California. While there, she was "discovered" by photographer David Conover, who convinced her to try modeling. This, of course, led to bleached blonde hair, three husbands, and worldwide fame!

School principals across the United States decided to ban jeans. Some schools even produced instructional brochures or short films showing appropriate dress for school (below-the-knee skirts for girls, dress pants for boys, blazers and dress shirts for everyone) and inappropriate clothing choices (mainly jeans). In Britain, a vicar banned jeans from his church youth group, claiming that anyone who wore jeans was a person whose

THE 1950s: JEANS WERE THERE

The 1950s brought dramatic scientific changes to the world. The Soviet Union launched Sputnik 1, the first man-made satellite, into space. American professor Jonas Salk invented a vaccine to prevent polio, and the first laser was unveiled. Many 1950s inventions seemed to celebrate Americans' social life and sense of fun: the telephone answering machine, the hula hoop, Mr. Potato Head. The same relaxed attitudes that inspired these inventions led more and more young people to pull on blue jeans.

Meanwhile, television was bringing news and pop culture right into people's homes. In living rooms and dance clubs, young people were moving to the first rock 'n' roll songs as Elvis Presley emerged as a star, crooning his way into teenage hearts and wiggling his blue-jean-clad hips.

morals were "practically non-existent."

Levi Strauss & Co. reacted with a 1957 advertisement, hoping to convince parents and teachers that jeans were suitable for teenagers. In the ad, a clean-cut young man wearing jeans, an Oxford shirt, and loafers carried an armload of books toward his classes. Alongside the photo blazed the words *Right for School!*

The company immediately received irate letters from parents. One mother from Hillsdale, New Jersey, wrote that the kind of behavior shown in the ad might be acceptable in the West, but it certainly wasn't appropriate in the East. She felt that school was serious and denim was much too casual. "I refer," she wrote, "to the picture showing a young boy dressed in shirt sleeves, sloppily opened at the collar and wearing dungarees…" Of course, all the debate about whether or not jeans were appropriate only made them more popular with teens.

The question of where jeans could or should be worn affected women as well. In 1954, a U.S. Army colonel in Germany asked the soldiers' wives to stop wearing jeans, telling them it gave Americans a poor image. He believed that Europeans would think the women were being too casual, or even too sexy. In his mind, jeans simply weren't appropriate for modest, married women.

In an attempt to convince parents and teachers that jeans were acceptable clothing for school (and not a sign that teens were running wild), Levi Strauss & Co. ran this ad in the late 1950s.

Teens on the Scene

There was no stopping the growth in jeans' popularity. Stars continued wearing them in movies and on TV, newspaper and magazine ads showed models dressed in jeans, and store windows showcased the latest styles. There were so many teens who were so in love with their jeans that schools and parents were eventually forced to adjust. After all, there were more kids now than ever before. Between the mid-1940s and the mid-1960s, about 76 million children were born in the U.S., and in 1957 alone a baby was born every seven seconds. In Britain the baby boom generation numbered more than 18 million, and in Canada the birth rate jumped by almost 20 percent.

By the 1960s, some of these post-war kids were starting to grow up. *Newsweek* magazine ran a feature article in 1963 called "The Teenagers: A Newsweek Survey of What They're Really Like." The magazine's cover showed a young girl wearing Wranglers, posed on the back of a motorcycle.

According to the article, there were 18 million teenagers in the United States and 76 percent of them liked to shop. Girls were spending $2 billion a year on clothes. That was information that perked the ears of the country's blue jeans makers. It was time to leave the last bits of workwear reputation behind and promote jeans as fun, stylish, and *young*. Billions of dollars depended on it. Of course, the companies had already been marketing to teens, but now, to please young customers, they began to make changes. After years of calling its pants "overalls" (the traditional name for men's work pants), Levi Strauss & Co. finally labeled the pants what everyone was calling them anyway: jeans.

In the late 1960s and early 1970s, hippies protested the Vietnam War and young people rebelled against the American government, their parents, and anything else that seemed old-fashioned. These new activists took the bad-boy image of jeans in the 1950s and went a step further, wearing denim as a way of rejecting their parents' business suits and money-centered lifestyles. Marshall McLuhan, a writer who specialized in exploring North American culture, said that "Jeans

You have to look for the "W" because it's silent Wrangler® the wreal jeans

More independent and rebellious than previous generations, the teenagers of the 1960s became the biggest new market for blue jeans. Companies like Wrangler appealed to the desire to look hip in the latest styles.

represent a rip off and a rage against the establishment." At Woodstock, a huge outdoor concert that drew more than half a million young people and anti-war protesters, thousands wore jeans. There were only two ways to look cool at Woodstock: wear your jeans or go naked.

THE 1960s: JEANS WERE THERE

By the 1960s there were 85 million TV sets in the U.S. The British rock group the Beatles drew screaming crowds to sold-out concerts. Girls wore miniskirts and psychedelic clothes, boxer Muhammad Ali rose to stardom, and Neil Armstrong became the first person to walk on the moon.

From students and music fans to hippies and protesters, everyone was wearing jeans. They were becoming such a visible part of North American culture that the Smithsonian Institution, the world's largest museum, added Levi's jeans to its collection in 1964.

To teens, the era was all about freedom—freedom to express yourself, to think differently than your parents, to dress differently than your friends. Having your own personal style was one way to prove that you were unique, so teens began altering or individualizing their jeans. Some embroidered the denim with flowers, some painted on peace symbols, some tie-dyed the fabric, and others cut open the seams and inserted colorful cotton strips. Personalized jeans became so popular that in 1973, Levi Strauss & Co. sponsored a denim art contest. The company received photographs of 2,000 pairs from the United States, Canada, and the Bahamas, each pair decorated with sequins, paint, or embroidery thread. The winning jeans were gathered into an exhibit that toured several American museums. Eventually, Levi Strauss & Co. bought some of the most unusual pairs for the company archives.

It didn't take long for the marketing departments at jeans companies to see the potential in decorated jeans. Soon factories were producing bell-bottomed jeans, jeans with fancy stitching, and patterned denim.

The world was changing quickly, and jeans were changing just as fast. In only a generation, blue jeans had gone from safe to psychedelic; they'd transformed into a hip, rebellious choice for teens. Where could they go next?

NO JEANS ALLOWED

In 1951, singer Bing Crosby arrived at a Canadian hotel in jeans. The hotel refused to allow him inside. When Levi Strauss & Co. learned of the incident, it produced a tuxedo jacket tailored specifically for Crosby— and made entirely of denim.

The artwork on this pair of 1974 jeans made them personal and political. The word *Watergate* near the waistband refers to a government scandal and suggests the designer wasn't a fan of U.S. president Richard Nixon.

CHAPTER 4

THE JEAN SCENE

Denim Gets Sexy on the Catwalks

By the 1970s, jeans had wiggled their way onto teenage behinds around the world. Just as North Americans fell in love with denim after World War II, so did European and Asian teens. Departing North American soldiers had left some of their clothes behind in Europe and Japan. Jeans were suddenly available at military surplus stores and became a hot look for the fashion-savvy.

And just as stars such as Marilyn Monroe had made jeans hot in North America, Brigitte Bardot gave them sex appeal in Europe. Bardot had begun modeling in 1949, when she was 15 years old. When she made the move to the big screen in the 1950s, many of her films showed daring glimpses of skin. Then she slipped on jeans for press appearances or star-studded parties. Instantly, denim left its army reputation behind and became the newest sexy trend.

For American companies, the new worldwide love affair with denim was a dream come true. Suddenly there were millions of international consumers clamoring to buy jeans, and Europe's clothing companies were slow to start producing them. The Lee Company moved quickly, opening an international division in New York City and its first overseas operation, a factory in Belgium. By the end of the 1960s, Lee jeans were being sold in Scotland, Spain, Australia, Brazil, and Hong Kong.

Levi Strauss & Co. wasn't far behind, exhibiting at a Paris show in 1961, creating Levi Strauss International in 1965, and opening Levi Strauss Japan in 1971. Wrangler jeans hit the world market in 1962, when the company opened a plant in Belgium. The globe-trotting pants were no longer just jeans. They became *pantalones vaqueros* (in Spanish), *calças de brim* (in Portuguese), and even *spijkerbroek* (in Dutch).

Black Market Jeans

A young traveler in Moscow explores the unfamiliar streets. He stops at a café for a break and is thrilled when a few Russian men introduce themselves and sit down to chat. Soon they're sharing a bottle of vodka. They have two drinks, then three, then four… Wait a second—how did he get outside? Where is his hotel? And where are his pants?! The traveler finds himself wandering the streets dressed in only his underwear.

This story may sound far-fetched, but it's exactly what happened to a Norwegian tourist in 1979. His new

Even when Communist Russia was supposedly closed to foreign companies, shoppers who were willing to pay enough could find the Western brands they craved. Photographed in 1983, the young man on the left at the Pepsi stand is wearing American jeans.

BEHIND THE IRON CURTAIN: JEANS WERE THERE

Soon after World War II, the developed world divided between democratic countries such as Great Britain, France, West Germany, and the U.S., and Communist countries such as the USSR, East Germany, and Poland.

In 1946, British politician Sir Winston Churchill said, "From Stettin in the Baltic to Trieste in the Adriatic, an iron curtain has descended across the continent." He meant that the Communist countries had isolated their citizens by restricting trade, censoring the news, and limiting travel. From behind this "iron curtain," European young people yearned for such things as music records, blue jeans, and fast-food hamburgers. To many, American popular culture represented freedom.

Russian "friends" turned out to be interested only in his blue jeans.

Denim companies were busily expanding around the world in the 1970s, but they weren't welcome everywhere. In Communist countries such as the USSR, government officials saw blue jeans as a corrupting force. They believed that buying Western goods such as jeans and rock music records would lure young people away from Communism and toward capitalism. They also believed that popular culture promoted poor morals; tight-fitting jeans were one more symbol of American corruption. Some politicians called the influx of Western goods and ideas a "plague." They refused to allow Levi's or Lee's to be imported, and suggested that the government use propaganda to turn teens against denim. Posters or newspaper articles, for example, could inform teens that jeans were part of a misguided, money-driven culture.

But when jeans were locked out at the front door, they snuck in through the back. Smugglers made thousands of dollars bringing denim across closed borders. A single pair could sell for a month's wages in Russia. In Yugoslavia in 1977, police arrested bootleggers trying to bring 1,200 pairs of jeans into the country – jeans that might have sold for up to US$100 a pair if they had made it onto the streets.

Smuggling was also undertaken on a smaller scale. Western tourists on vacation in Russia could often help fund their trip by taking along a few extra pairs of Levi's. Some experts believe that in the late 1970s, about 10,000 pairs of jeans a year were secretly imported by black marketers, and another 100,000 pairs arrived in the country with tourists, foreign students, and business people.

Vacationers who weren't willing to part with their pants could find Russian young people less than friendly. The Norwegian who was robbed of his jeans in Moscow wasn't the only traveler to find himself in trouble. In one Soviet city, members of a youth league once chased a young man through the streets, demanding his pants. When he refused to hand them over, he was stabbed. In the same incident, teenage girls used knives and razor blades to attack two other people and steal their jeans.

Unable to stop illegal blue jeans from flowing across the border, some East German officials decided on a different strategy: they would try to make money from the trend. After all, if jeans could sell for so much on the black market, why shouldn't the government get a share of the profit?

In 1978, the East German government ordered 800,000 pairs of jeans from Levi Strauss & Co. The pants were flown across the border, and East German young people lined up at store counters across the country, hoping to get the "real thing." Each shopper was allowed to buy one pair, for the equivalent of more than US$70. Since the government had purchased the pants for $11.25 a pair, there was plenty of profit to be made.

In Hungary, the Communist government was more flexible about importing jeans to meet the demands of young people. In 1977, a million pairs were sold through stores. Eventually, four Hungarian companies negotiated with Levi Strauss & Co. to be able to produce jeans for the Eastern European market. The jeans were in stores by 1979, bearing the all-important Levi's label on the back pocket.

Why were jeans so popular behind the Iron Curtain? Not only were they symbols of Western freedom, they were signs of wealth and power within Communist society. People who wore jeans had traveled overseas, had access to the American cash needed to buy black-market goods, or had rich and influential friends.

Jeans with European Genes

Jeans were growing increasingly popular around the world, not just behind the Iron Curtain. By 1977, shoppers in West Germany alone were spending US$800 million each year on denim. Obviously, it was time for jeans companies to go big or go home. Wrangler opened more European factories to meet the demand.

In 1983, the first Original Levi's Store opened in Spain, and hundreds

COKE VS. MAVI

Based in Turkey, Mavi is one of Europe's most successful jeans companies. In 2003, Mavi was the second most recognized brand name in Turkey, following only Coca-Cola.

more followed in countries from Germany to Japan. In fact, Levi's were so popular in Germany that in 1990 the company won the German Apparel Supplier of the Year award—the first non-German company to do so.

Meanwhile, a few European companies had been producing their own versions of blue jeans. After all, the patent on riveted pants had expired way back in 1891, and there was nothing to stop companies around the world from trying to capture a piece of the market. But while some European designs—including tight-fitting styles—were popular, it was decades before a brand other than Levi's, Lee, or Wrangler really cashed in.

In 1991, a Turkish textile company launched its own label—Mavi Jeans—in Istanbul. (*Mavi* means "blue" in Turkish.) Within three years Mavi was selling jeans throughout Europe, and by 1998 it was exporting a million pairs a year to customers from Canada to Croatia. Huge U.S. department stores, including Nordstrom and Bloomingdales, were carrying the pants, and such celebrities as Chelsea Clinton and Cher were wearing Mavis.

Designer Denim

In 1977, a member of the state legislature in Texas proposed that jeans be declared the official state clothing. Denim had already been immortalized in songs such as the 1956 release "The Blue Jean Bop." When Neil Diamond sang "Forever in Blue Jeans" in 1978, it topped the charts.

Andy Warhol was an artist famous in the 1970s for painting seemingly ordinary bits of North American culture. In the decade before, he had painted a Campbell's soup can, bottles of Coca-Cola, and portraits of celebrities like Marilyn Monroe. In 1971, the rock group the Rolling Stones asked Warhol to design a cover for their newest album, *Sticky Fingers*. Warhol's creation featured a photograph of jeans. Attached to the image was a real, working zipper. In the 1980s, Bruce Springsteen's album *Born in the U.S.A.* sported a cover featuring his rear, clad in denim.

If rock stars were wearing them, jeans had obviously hit the big time. And denim's new glamour meant there was room for something new. Something flashy. Something... designer.

In 1979, a clothing maker called Murjani Corporation approached Gloria Vanderbilt, a famous heiress, artist, and clothing designer. The corporation proposed that Gloria lend her name to a new line of blue jeans. Tight-fitting and bearing Gloria's signature on the back pocket, the Gloria Vanderbilt jeans were a hit, opening a whole new market of upscale "designer" denim.

Other companies were quick to follow. Inspired by the tight-fitting European jeans, Jordache pioneered the "Jordache look" of sexy denim in the late 1970s. Calvin Klein raised

GOING BUGGY
In 1990 a company called Genencor made millions by perfecting a way to have bacteria munch away at denim, creating an aged, stone-washed look without the expensive pumice stone.

eyebrows with ads featuring teen star Brooke Shields. She sashayed onto the TV screen and purred, "You know what comes between me and my Calvins? Nothing," implying that she wasn't wearing any underwear. In magazine ads that appeared at the same time, she was shown posed in tight jeans, unbuttoning her shirt. The ads drew attention not only because they were so openly sexual but because Shields was only 15 years old. Critics accused Calvin Klein of exploiting a young girl. Some even called the ads child pornography. CBS and other TV stations banned the commercials, but the move only brought Calvin Klein more publicity. His ads may have been controversial, but they were hugely successful.

While Brooke Shields caused an uproar in 1980, we wouldn't look twice at the television commercial today. That's because Calvin Klein started a trend: using sex to sell a product. Soon rap star Marky Mark was posing in his boxer shorts and Claudia Schiffer was dancing in her Victoria's Secret underwear. Today we watch sexy TV commercials all the time and see semi-naked models on billboards whenever we drive through city streets—and nobody blinks.

On the Brand Wagon

Using sex appeal wasn't the only way that jeans companies tried to distinguish their brands. French designers Marithe and François Girbaud, for example, noticed that jeans were most loved once they'd been worn a few

THOSE ROCKS ROCKED!
At the height of the 1980s stonewashed craze, Lee employed 10,000 people at 17 sewing plants and 5 laundries, and could produce 200,000 pairs of jeans each day.

times, losing their "new blue" look. The couple set out to perfect a process to pre-age denim, destroying a few industrial-sized washing machines along the way. First they tried washing denim with sand, to no avail. Then they tried washing it with large rocks, a process that proved more expensive than effective. Finally they tried Italian pumice stone, a lava rock that actually floats in water. The result was denim with irregular faded patches—the "stonewashed" look was born!

Stonewashed jeans proved so popular throughout the 1980s that other companies attempted to develop their own versions. The Lee Company tried washing its denim with shredded rubber tires, bottle caps, golf balls, rope, and wood chips before finally settling on pumice stone as well. At one point Lee was spending $2 million a year buying rocks! When the company couldn't find the right variety in the United States, it imported stone from Turkey, Greece, and Mexico.

Other companies used bleach to wear down their denim. Manufacturers

Punk rock singers wore jeans with huge holes or tears. Like their dyed hair and tattoos, the jeans were meant to show that punks lived by their own standards, not the established rules of everyday society.

While the new Polo denim appealed to older shoppers, young people weren't interested in remembering cowboy days. The youth rebellions of the 1960s were reborn in the 1970s in the punk music groups of London and New York. Through their clothing and music, punks protested a world where everything seemed to be about manners and money. Their songs were hard-hitting looks at love, sex, and politics, and punks refused to change either their music or their looks to conform to the "acceptable" standard. They had spiked hair, dark makeup, torn or taped shirts, and ripped jeans.

Without going to the extremes of the punks, many teens found that wearing ripped jeans was the perfect way to express their own rebellious side, and annoy parents and teachers in the process. By the 1980s, ripped jeans had gone from a punk phenomenon to a teen trend, and jeans companies began noticing. Marithe and François Girbaud were the first designers to intentionally tear their new denim, calling their pre-ripped pants "destroyed jeans." Other companies followed the fad. An American firm called Jou Jou took a backlog of plain, boring styles and started ripping them; the jeans soon sold out.

in Italy and the United States simultaneously developed a method of soaking pumice stones in bleach, then adding them to a dryer full of denim to create random bleach spots—a look they called "acid-washed."

Not every company tried to reinvent denim. When Ralph Lauren added jeans to his Polo clothing line in 1978, he paired the denim with leather vests and jackets, patterned skirts, and fringed buckskin to celebrate cowboy history. Fashion critics loved the look, writing that he had "recaptured America for America." Ralph Lauren was so pleased with the new line that he appeared in the ads himself, dressed for the Wild West.

Wearing the New Wave

Jeans had once been one-shape-fits-all garments, meant to last forever. Farm workers hadn't stood in changing rooms gazing into three-way mirrors and asking, "Do these pants make my butt look big?" They had simply bought a new pair that looked almost exactly like the pair they had bought the year before, and the year before that.

The introduction of designer denim changed the market. Now there was a different style for every body type. People began to distinguish between their "good jeans"—the new, fashionable ones they'd bought the month before—and their "old jeans"—the ones from last year with holes in the knees. There were now plain, straight-leg cuts for moms and dads, and creatively dyed or studded styles for teens. Jeans became fashion statements, with new designers constantly offering up their own visions.

One of these visions was the Marilyn jean by Guess?, a tight, sexy style with zippers at the ankles. Department store managers didn't think the style would catch on. In fact, they didn't think their customers were even looking for jeans. Boy, were they wrong! When Bloomingdales was finally convinced to order 24 pairs, they sold out within hours. By focusing on new styles and searching for the world's most seductive models, including Anna Nicole Smith and Claudia Schiffer, Guess? combined jeans with sex appeal. Just as Calvin Klein had learned with his hot Brooke Shields commercials, Guess? found that sexy ads sold more jeans.

With people craving new styles every season, designers were continuously looking for inspiration. In 1987, Salvatore Parasuco of Parasuco Jeans hired someone to sandblast the company logo into the door of his office. He wondered

GUESS WHAT?

Guess? was founded by four brothers, the Marcianos. On his first trip to America, Georges Marciano passed a McDonald's billboard on Olympic Boulevard in Los Angeles. The ad read, "GUESS what is in the new Big Mac?" Georges knew he'd found the perfect name for the brothers' new company.

aloud if the sandblasting machine could be used on jeans.

"Are you crazy?" the worker asked.

Maybe Salvatore was a tad off-kilter: he rented a sandblasting machine and tried it himself. When he sent the results to the laundry, he told people that the fabric was new, and imported directly from Italy; he didn't want anyone stealing his sandblasting ideas. The jeans sold for $65 a pair and were just one of the chic designs that led to Parasuco opening showrooms in Montreal, New York, Los Angeles, and Milan.

By the 1990s there were hundreds of jeans variations—tight, baggy, dark, faded, boot-cut, bell-bottomed, beaded. There was a different pair for everyone's taste and budget—especially if that budget happened to be huge. A Roberto Cavalli design with a beaded waistband went for a whopping US$1,840. Gucci jeans with torn knees were showcased on fashion runways in 1999 and instantly sold out. They were $3,715 a pair.

The divide-and-conquer strategy was successful. Even though they couldn't

It's hard to keep your hands to yourself when your friends' jeans are so hot. At least that's the message behind ads like this one that use sex appeal to sell pants.

shell out thousands of dollars, 13-to-17-year-old shoppers became the number one buyers of denim, and many were willing to pay up to $150 for a pair of Levi's.

Behind Bars

Not all new designers were looking for the upscale fashion market. For years, a sewing department inside the Eastern Oregon Correction Institution had been making uniforms and jeans for inmates. In 1997 the jailhouse began marketing its Prison Blues line to shoppers under the motto "Made on the Inside to be Worn on the Outside."

Jailhouse jeans sparked another trend. Because prisoners weren't allowed to have belts (or anything else that could be used to hurt themselves or others), they wore their jeans loose around the hips. The style was soon picked up by urban teens, including big-name rap stars. For many of the rappers, success depended on a bad-boy reputation: they had to look as if they'd done hard time in prison (and a few of them had). Their baggy, low-rise jeans were a part of this image. As television and music videos took rap and hip hop from the inner cities to the suburbs, the fashion traveled too. The traditional rise (the distance from the waistband to the crotch) on a pair of men's jeans was about 30 centimeters (12 inches). Now guys were looking for low-slung pants with a rise of about 20 centimeters (8 inches). They wore them low around the hips, with the waistband of their underwear showing.

In the early 1990s, hip-hop-inspired styles were available only in a few big-city stores. Then music stars like Russell Simmons and Sean (P. Diddy) Combs started designing their own lines of menswear, and low-rise jeans and oversized shirts became available in every North American mall.

Always watching for new trends, Levi Strauss & Co. released the Dangerously Low line of jeans for men. Diesel Jeans also released men's hip-huggers, and snagged a huge publicity boost when Brad Pitt started wearing his to Hollywood events.

Jeans were more popular than ever. Or were they? Teen buyers still eyed the latest denim trends, but they had other issues on their minds as well—issues such as globalization and fair trade. At the end of the 20th century, some people began looking at jeans from a different angle, and they didn't always like what they found below the belt.

CHAPTER 5

BORDERLESS BLUES

What's Happening Behind the Hype

There are politics in pants. Until the 1990s, most teens had never stopped to think about who sewed their jeans, where in the world they lived, and whether or not they were fairly paid. But every time they read the label on a waistband, they were making choices. Were they buying from a company that helped protect the environment, paid workers a living wage, and avoided child labor? Or were they paying discount prices because a 12-year-old sewed their seams? Before they opened their wallets, shoppers began wondering who was pocketing the cash.

Cotton-pickin' Problems

One problem with jeans begins long before the factory floor. It starts with a shrub planted in the fields of the southern United States, China, India, Pakistan, Uzbekistan, Turkey, and more than 50 other countries. Cotton, the plant used to make denim fibers, is grown on 34 million hectares (84 million acres) around the world.

Unfortunately, cotton doesn't appeal only to clothing makers. It also draws boll weevils, army worms, thrips, red spiders, boll-worms, and tobacco budworms, which have followed their favorite food to fields all over the world. Because cotton attracts so many insects, cotton farmers rely on huge amounts of chemicals to protect their crops. In fact, they use almost a quarter of the world's insecticides each year. In countries where the methods of pesticide application are unsafe, workers sometimes die from chemical exposure.

Cotton crops also require water—a lot of it. In Uzbekistan, cotton growers desperate for irrigation have partly drained a huge inland sea, leaving fishing villages stranded far from shore. Fishing vessels sit marooned on the sand, and even if they could be moved closer to the shrunken sea, there are few fish left to find. The water that still manages to find its way there has picked up pesticides along its route, killing the local wildlife. Most of the cotton is exported; there are few clothing factories in Uzbekistan. Many of the people who live there have never owned jeans, and some have never even seen a pair.

It's possible to grown cotton without using pesticides, but it's more expensive. At present, organic cotton is rarely used by the world's large jeans makers.

PLANTS WITH PEDIGREE

Cotton is one of the oldest crops in the world. It's been grown in Mexico for at least 7,000 years and in India for at least 5,000. It was also used by the ancient people of China, Egypt, and South America—and grown without pesticides, of course. The first North American settlers planted cotton in 1607.

On the Factory Floor

If you could walk through an early jeans factory, you would probably be shocked. Hundreds of teenagers sat side by side in wooden chairs at long trestle tables, bent over sewing machines or operating button punches. They labored ten hours each day, six days a week, and worked overtime whenever the company was especially busy. If they were hurt at work, they had to pay for their own doctor or medication. If they were lucky, they would get their jobs back when they recovered.

Sound barbaric? The way companies are required to treat their workers in North America and Europe has drastically changed since the 19th century. As early as the 1930s, workers began to band together in unions and demand better working conditions and fair pay. Seamstresses campaigned for higher wages and African-Americans pushed for equal rights. Slowly, these labor groups persuaded governments to pass laws that protected workers.

The people who worked 60-hour weeks in the factory in the late 1800s would find their lives much different today. They would be paid at least a minimum wage, and earn overtime if they worked more than 40 hours in a week. In fact, under today's laws, most of those teenagers wouldn't be allowed to work full-time in the first place—they would be attending school instead.

Behind the Seams

Check the labels on your blue jeans. Were they sewn in the United States? Canada? Britain? Probably not. Jeans may have been born in North America, but they aren't made here much any more. Because of the rising costs of labor, many jeans companies moved their factories to developing countries in the 1980s and 1990s. Australia used to produce more than half of its own jeans; now it makes less than a third.

Some American jeans companies simply moved their factories across the border from California to Mexico. While workers in California had been making $10 or $12 per hour, workers in Mexico could be found for as little as $7 per day. The city of Tehuacán, Mexico, has the lowest minimum wage in the nation and is home to 700 clothing manufacturing companies. The industry earns $450 million each year, and blue jeans are the most popular product made there.

This employee at a jeans factory in San Francisco was likely paid about half of what male workers earned. Seamstresses in the 19th century often worked sixteen-hour days, six or even seven days a week.

Labor activists say workers in Mexico are poorly paid, badly treated, and sometimes exposed to toxic dyes and chemicals. Factories in Torreón, Mexico, make about 6 million garments a week and export most of them to Canada and the United States.

Wages are just as low—or lower—in other countries. In Honduras, a woman sewing clothes for export might make US$139 a month, and in parts of China, about $64. In Bangladesh, a similar worker makes just over $18 each month.

Sometimes, overseas production means not only lower wages but lower workplace standards. An American delegation that went to the island of Saipan in the South Pacific to investigate factory conditions found some people there working almost as slaves. Recruiters had charged these people up to $7,000 to get them a factory job, then forced them to work in bondage until the "debt" was paid off. Companies buying clothes made at these questionable factories included at least two major American jeans makers.

Back in 2003, a New York–based labor group brought a worker from a Honduran sweatshop to Manhattan. They staged a protest outside the store of a popular designer jeans maker, claiming that the jeans being sold inside were made in sweatshops where workers were treated unfairly. People who had arrived to shop at the store stayed outside on the sidewalk instead, listening as the 19-year-old girl described her factory, where the workers were limited to two bathroom breaks a day and were forced to work overtime without pay. They weren't allowed to talk to each other, in case they slowed down or tried to start a union. They were also regularly tested for pregnancy and HIV. Workers who tested positive were fired.

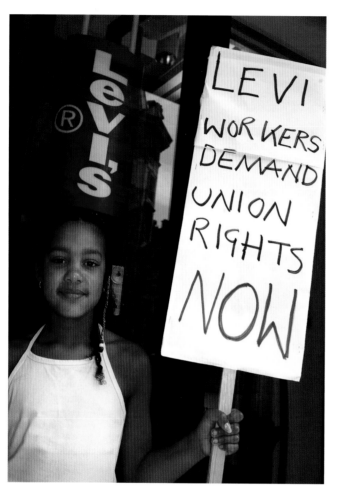

This protester in London, England, was speaking out for people half a world away. Workers at a Levi's subcontractor in Haiti were threatened by their bosses and beaten by armed guards when they tried to form a union in March 2004. By April, Levi Strauss & Co. had met with labor activists and the factory owners had agreed to recognize the workers' rights.

As the young woman continued to speak, reporters began to join the crowd of would-be shoppers. By the next day the worker's story had made newspaper headlines and the company was rethinking the way it handed out contracts.

Sweatshop Shock

Sweatshops don't operate only in developing countries. In 1995, police raided an apartment complex in El Monte, California, where they found 72 Thai immigrants sewing clothes for 69 cents an hour. The workers had been smuggled into the country and threatened with murder if they quit working or escaped before they "repaid" the smugglers for bringing them to the United States. Some of the immigrants had been held there for more than two years.

Many Americans were shocked by the news of sweatshops operating in their own country, but a 1994 government study had found that half of the clothing factories in Los Angeles paid less than minimum wage, and more than 90 percent broke health and safety laws.

Stirring the Protest Pot

In the 1990s, the Union of Needletrades, Industrial and Textile Employees (UNITE) accused Guess? of using sweatshop labor in developing countries and staged protests in front of many Guess? stores.

Similar protests struck The Gap. In 1995, a worker from El Salvador stood in front of a Gap store in Toronto and told shoppers that she worked in a contractor's sweatshop, where she was paid 27 cents per item to sew shirts that later sold for $34.

Guess? and The Gap denied any knowledge of sweatshop conditions, claiming that they simply contracted with independent companies for their clothing. But that explanation didn't satisfy demonstrators. Almost all the major jeans makers found themselves ducking controversy as shoppers became more aware of the sweatshop labor used around the world.

Changing Their Jeans

The oldest jeans companies had spent a century and a half advertising their products as symbols of American liberty. Companies like The Gap relied on images of fun and freedom. Guess? campaigns had always been sexy. Because of these associations, the jeans companies were vulnerable to public opinion. It was hard for shoppers to feel sexy or free in their jeans after hearing about slave labor or beaten workers.

In 1991, Levi Strauss & Co. reacted by releasing a code of conduct requiring all contractors in other countries to treat workers fairly. Company em-

WOULD YOU COUGH UP THE CASH?

Would you be willing to pay extra for your jeans to guarantee they weren't sewn in a sweatshop? A survey of Canadians in 1995 showed that shoppers would be willing to pay 10 percent more if their clothes were made by well-treated and well-paid workers.

ployees also began monitoring foreign factories. Guess? launched a major anti-sweatshop campaign in 1997, labeling its clothing with tags that read, "This is a no-sweat garment." The Gap went even further and agreed to have independent reviewers monitor its factories.

None of this means that workers in China or Mexico are suddenly earning big bucks, but hopefully they can now buy food. And are regular bathroom breaks too much to ask?

No-sweat Choices

Jeans makers depend on millions of young shoppers choosing to buy their jeans every day. That gives teens the power to influence how these companies operate.

How can you be sure you're buying jeans made in respectable factories? You can't tell whether jeans were made in

Bangladesh or Burma by holding the denim up to a light, but you can start by reading the label, and you can often check the company website. Does the company supervise its contractors? Does it ban the use of child labor? Does it make unannounced visits to its factories to monitor safety standards? How does it deal with contractors that break the rules?

You won't find the answers to these questions on all company websites. If you can't find the information you're looking for, try e-mailing or writing the company's public relations department. When enough people write letters about their concerns, companies will listen. After all, teenagers are these companies' biggest market. Indirectly, teens control the blue jean world!

Inseam Issues

When jeans makers went global, they found cheap labor and something else: access to huge new markets. Soon, companies were competing hard to win the hearts of shoppers in Mexico, Brazil, and India. Major brands such as Levi's and Lee spent millions of dollars marketing their jeans both at home in North America and in Europe, Asia, and South America.

There are two ways to win a customer. The first: produce a colorful billboard, catch the eye of a passerby, and sell one pair of jeans. The second: create a string of ads that tie your jeans to a cool or sexy image; convince a shopper that he or she loves your product more than any other; finally, sell the same shopper a new pair of jeans three

DISTRESSING NEWS

Distressed jeans with faded patches, worn seams, or wrinkled patterns in the dye are a popular trend of the last few years. But the processes used to make these jeans can be downright dangerous. According to some reports, the creeks around Mexican factories turn blue from the dye used. And workers may be exposed to toxic fumes from the acids and bleaches used in the design process. For more information on how to buy "clean" jeans, check out the Maquila Solidarity Network website at www.maquilasolidarity.org.

years in a row. Called "creating brand loyalty," the second method of marketing allows companies to win customers for life. That's why, to jeans makers, counterfeit jeans spell disaster. If you bought a pair of Levi's that fell apart the first time you washed them, you'd likely choose another brand the next time you shopped. Or if you bought a pair of Levi's for $50 and a friend found a pair that looked identical at a local flea market for $5, you'd feel ripped off.

Of course, one reason jeans companies hate counterfeiting is that they lose money every time a fake pair is sold. But it's more than that. The low quality of some knock-off jeans damages the reputation of the real brand. And when fake pairs are available to shoppers, the price of the real thing goes down. When the International Trademark Association surveyed its members, including Levi Strauss & Co., it found that companies lost an average of $2 billion a year because of counterfeiting. Even when you're rich—*really* rich—a missing $2 billion leaves a big hole in your bank account.

The smuggling of counterfeit jeans is nothing new. In the 1970s, Swiss and Dutch police cracked a smuggling ring

According to the activist group Maquila Solidarity Network, jeans factories in Mexico are dumping toxic chemicals into the groundwater. Factories pour leftover dye into the Valsequillo Canal between the cities of Puebla and Tehuacán—the same canal that farmers downstream use to irrigate their crops.

If you visited Saudi Arabia, you might see American jeans chains and slick, modern advertising, but you would rarely see a pair of jeans worn on the street. Many men there wear long robe-like garments, and women don't venture outside without putting floor-length cloaks over their clothes.

that began in Taiwan. There, factories made cheap jeans and sewed on fake Levi's labels. The smugglers then shipped 30,000 pairs to Switzerland and 22,000 pairs to a warehouse in Amsterdam. The police nabbed four ringleaders—seemingly "respectable" business people from Germany, Holland, Italy, and Great Britain—just as they were about to sneak the shipment of 30,000 pairs from Switzerland into West Germany.

So, let's see… First you take jeans companies that produce jeans overseas, then you add foreign factory owners who learn to make them, and presto: an explosion of counterfeit pants. Surely the jeans companies could have predicted the problem.

It's too late now. Some experts in Chinese trade estimate that up to one-fifth of all goods sold in China are counterfeit. With 6,000 shipping containers from China arriving in the U.S. each day and even more going to Europe, that's a lot of fake jeans that could be slipping across borders.

In 1995, Levi Strauss & Co. sued a company for making thousands of pairs of fake Levi's in China and

DIRTY JEANS

Unions around the world are struggling to improve working conditions in clothing factories. The ITGLWF (International Textile, Garment and Leather Workers' Federation) doesn't promote boycotting specific clothing manufacturers, because the boycotts may put fair factories out of work along with the irresponsible ones. Instead, the union, through the Global Union Federation, has produced a "blacklist" of factories that have broken work and safety standards again and again. Calling its list the Register of Dirty Companies, the Federation asks jeans makers to take their business elsewhere.

shipping them to Europe. (In other words, they "sued the pants off them"!) In 2004, agents with U.S. Immigration and Customs Enforcement arrested twelve people and seized six shipping containers packed with fake jeans, sweatshirts, purses, and other products. The agency estimated that the smugglers had brought $400 million worth of counterfeit goods into the U.S. in the past year.

Fake jeans are also made in North America. In September 2004, police arrested five people in New Jersey and confiscated $500,000 worth of merchandise. The counterfeiters had bought pairs of generic jeans, sewed on fake designer labels, and sold them at flea markets.

Obviously, jeans company presidents have new problems to keep them awake at night. How can they make affordable pants without abusing workers, find loyal customers in countries around the world, and protect their valuable brands from counterfeiters?

And how can they lure shoppers toward a shiny rack of brand new jeans when those same shoppers already have five other pairs at home?

THE REAL DEAL

How can you be sure that your pants are the real thing and not cheap knock-offs? Jeans companies offer the following advice: shop at established stores, not flea markets; look for distinguishing features like the leather patch on Lee waistbands; and remember that if the price seems too good to be true, it probably is.

CHAPTER 6

PANTING FOR PERFECTION

21st-century Trends

Warning! Do NOT sit down on your aunt's brand new white leather couch. Why? Because the jeans you bought yesterday are infused with so much dark blue dye that it's rubbing off on the furniture. In fact, if you stand in the rain before you wash these jeans, your skin will temporarily turn blue.

It may sound over-the-top, but it's true. Jeans companies are trying so hard to find new styles that each season brings us a strange new option. One month we wear denim with faded yellow patches on the thighs; the next month we're wearing faded black hip-huggers with the pockets low on our behind. Brands offer more style choices than ever before, they market their pants in as many countries as possible, and they bombard buyers with ads. Why? Because shoppers can always be tempted by the promise of something new.

The Jailbird Blues

Sometimes our love of unique styles gives small companies a leg up (literally).

Because it doesn't have a big-name image to protect, a small company can make a big splash. Take Haeftling, for example, a brand made in Germany's largest prison. Prisoners had sewn their own uniforms at Berlin's Tegel Prison since the 1800s and had sold clothes through a small shop nearby. For years the salespeople there had smiled innocently at shoppers and said, "These clothes are made by local craftspeople," or "The sewers come from different backgrounds." Basically, they had done everything possible to avoid the truth: the clothes were made by convicts.

In 2003, a Berlin advertising agency convinced the prison to change its approach. The agency launched a new website, and christened shoes, briefcases, and denim jackets with the word *Haeftling*, which means "inmate" in German. Within two weeks the prison had received 3,000 orders. When it comes to jeans, a bad image can be a good thing!

Wabi/Sabi

Ironically, the quest to wear something new and different has sometimes led shoppers to rediscover the past. In Japan, there's a concept known as wabi/sabi—the idea that the value of something comes partly from its flaws. Picture your favorite pair of jeans. Even though you've worn them several hundred times and a belt loop is missing and the seams are frayed, you still put them on when you want to feel completely comfortable. And that little rip in the knee? That just reminds you of the party where you ripped it (and

met the love of your life) and makes the jeans even more precious. That's the idea behind wabi/sabi.

In the early 1990s, Japanese shoppers began to see beauty in the flaws of old American jeans. Suddenly, Levi's and Lee's from the 1940s, '50s, and '60s were the hottest goods at the local street markets. Dealers and buyers learned to identify the age of jeans by the selvage or inside seams, by minute changes to the labels, or by the stitching on the back pockets. A specific style of used

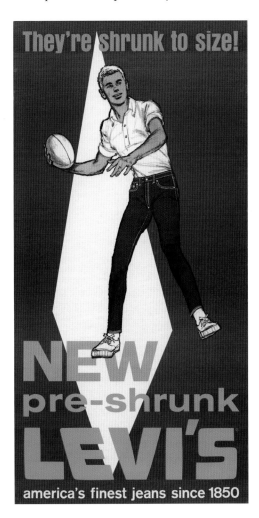

They're shrunk to size!

NEW pre-shrunk LEVI'S

america's finest jeans since 1850

Jeans are constantly evolving as companies think up improvements and new marketing angles. This ad from the 1960s introduces pre-shrunk Levi's. No more jumping into horse troughs to shrink the denim to fit!

Salesman Chester Reynolds made the first Buddy Lee doll in 1920. Since then, the company mascot has appeared in all sorts of outfits, from a railroad engineer's suit to cowboy gear. Collectors pay up to $1,000 for some of the oldest dolls.

they received bids as high as $30,000. Even jeans memorabilia gained value. Buddy Lee (the Lee brand mascot) dolls sold for hundreds of times what they originally cost. In 1994, a Paris auction offered an antique Levi Strauss & Co. promotional item—a cardboard cutout of a cowboy wearing 501s. Bidding reached 130,000 francs, the equivalent of about US$75,000 at the time.

Obviously, it was time for old to become new again. Or for new to become old. In 2002, the *New York Times Magazine* interviewed a New Yorker named Troy Pierce. Troy had a favorite pair of jeans, which he wore to work, to ride his motorcycle, and even out to the clubs at night. He rarely washed them. A Levi's jeans designer named Sun Choe happened to spot Troy in his tattered pants and immediately fell in love (with the jeans, not the guy). She took the stained and smelly pants back to her design team and used them as inspiration for a new look. Levi Strauss & Co. and other jeans companies also cashed in on the vintage market by making new jeans from worn denim. Diesel and Ralph Lauren sold their versions for $150 or $200 a pair.

Levi's—marked by a big E on the red tab—could sell for up to $1,500. And when old clothes become that valuable, they're no longer called old—they're "vintage."

After decades of exporting ideas to other countries, jeans companies took the craze for vintage jeans home to North America. A former Levi's salesperson found an unworn, unwashed pair of decades-old jeans stuffed in the back of his dresser drawer. He sold them to a vintage clothing store for $2,500. When the store resold the pants,

Customization Stations

What do small designer labels and vintage jeans have in common? Both allow shoppers to choose something different—something to distinguish themselves from friends. In August 1999, Levi Strauss & Co. opened a store in San Francisco where buyers could have their body scanned by beams of light that measured their waistline, their hips, and the length of their legs. Shoppers could then design their ideal pants on a computer screen, and the store would order them a custom-cut, perfectly fitted pair. By 2002, American Eagle was offering similar "customization stations," where shoppers could use stencils, razors, or pumice stones to individualize their purchases. From whiskered white creases on the thighs to lines of poetry in gold paint to fine embroidery, jeans soon had every finishing detail imaginable.

A company called Fractal Jeans recently pioneered a process that uses an industrial-sized, 2,500-watt laser to etch intricate patterns into jeans. For a price, Fractal even customizes specific pairs with their buyer's signature or favorite patterns. And in 2004, some shoppers joined a waiting list for jeans from a California company called Sadlelite, which created a limited number of pairs using denim hand-woven on antique Japanese looms.

So now we can have any style we want. We have our big and baggy, our hip and trendy, and our skin-tight and sexy jeans. We have our going-camping-

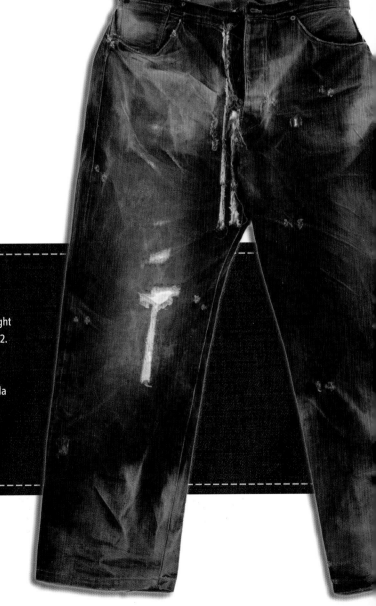

A MINER'S JEANS STRIKE IT RICH

In May 2001, Levi Strauss & Co. bought a pair of jeans from eBay for $46,532. They were obviously no ordinary jeans! The pants dated from 1880 and had been discovered in a Nevada mining town. Even after more than 100 years, the pants were still good as gold.

in-the-woods pair and our heading-to-the-dance-club pair. Could we possibly need more jeans? Yes, yes, yes! At least, that's what the jeans companies want us to believe. Billions of dollars depend on it.

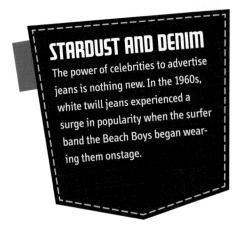

Ad-ing It All Up

We've all seen ads for the newest jeans trends on billboards, in magazines, or on bus shelters. But did you know that you might be watching an ad every time you tune in to your favorite music video or TV sitcom? Companies have discovered that putting their pants on celebrity butts is a good way to get attention. Rogan jeans became famous after appearing on *Friends*. Lucky Brand also concentrated on getting its

Brad Pitt and Gwyneth Paltrow walk the red carpet in jeans at a 1995 film premiere. In Japan, Pitt is famous for endorsing Edwin jeans. He mangled his Japanese pronunciation so badly in the first TV commercial that shoppers started imitating him, spawning a whole series of ads.

denim onto famous legs. The jeans were worn by the actors in *Friends, Buffy the Vampire Slayer*, and *Scream II*. Sometimes companies pay thousands or even millions of dollars for the privilege of placing their jeans in TV shows, movies, or rock videos. Occasionally they get lucky and a star simply decides to wear his or her favorite jeans in public.

Parasuco is a small Canadian company that has always managed to attract attention. In 2003, Salvatore Parasuco was convinced that the perfect spokesperson for his jeans was rocker Avril Lavigne. Her first CD had just sold more than 14 million copies and she was idolized by teenage girls around the world. What better person to advertise a pair of Parasuco pants? But Avril wasn't likely to sign on as an advertising model—she was someone who wore what she liked, when she liked. Also, Parasuco didn't have an advertising budget large enough to tempt a rock star.

Is this a photo of a rear end or a walking advertisement? Labels on the waistbands or back pockets of jeans act just like logos on the fronts of our T-shirts—they tell the world what brands we choose to "endorse."

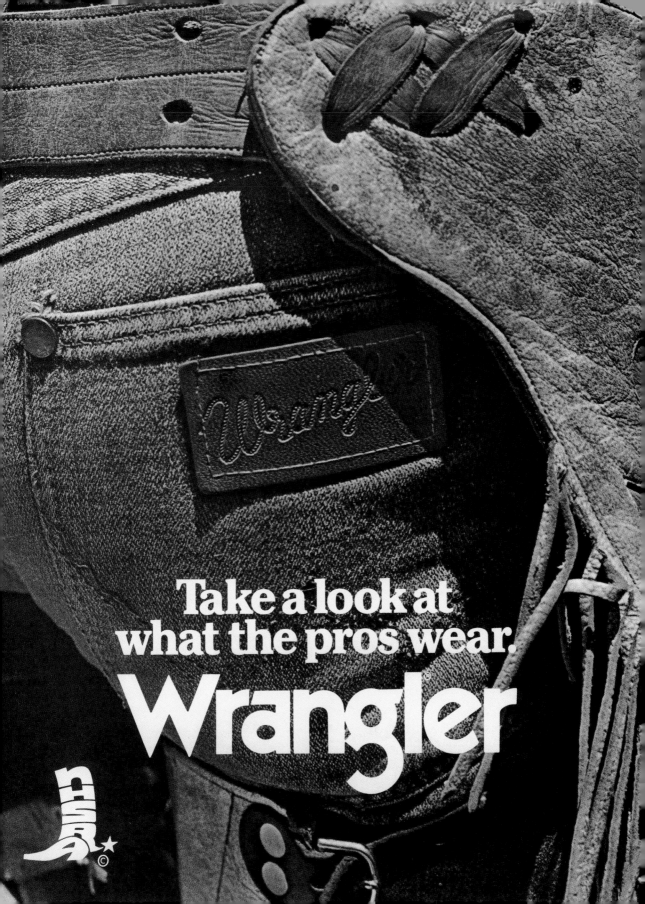

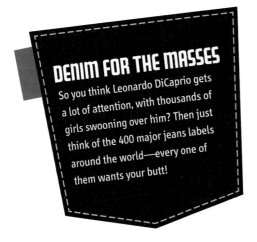

To catch Avril's attention, Salvatore, his marketing genius Tuti Do, and his designers spent weeks studying Avril's style and designing a pair of cargo pants just for her. They guessed at Avril's size, sent the pants to her manager, and waited for results. They weren't entirely hopeful.

For months there was no sign of the cargo pants. Then Parasuco received a call from Avril's manager. The Canadian flag on the waistband of the cargo pants had caught Avril's eye and she wanted to wear them to an awards show. When Avril's manager provided the star's exact measurements, Parasuco whipped up a brand new pair, happy to see them in front of a TV audience of 2.2 million.

Some companies, such as Wrangler, have had decades of practice using celebrities to endorse their jeans. Remember the rodeo stars and singing cowboys of the 1930s and 1940s? In 2004, Wrangler hired NASCAR driver Dale Earnhardt Jr. to star in its magazine and TV ads, hoping to associate Earnhardt's

energy and love for speed with "a new generation of Wrangler."

Hiring celebrities is just one way that denim companies spend millions—and millions and millions—of dollars to capture your attention. In 2002, Wrangler bought commercial time during college and NFL football games, and ran ads in *Sports Illustrated* and *People* magazines. The company was aiming for two markets: men, who bought more Wrangler jeans than women, and teens, who were buying 12 percent more jeans than ever before. The company's advertising budget for the year was $20 million. In 2003, it spent $32 million. Levi Strauss & Co., meanwhile, spent $15 million in 2003 on newspaper and magazine ads alone.

The Deeper Side of Denim

In Australia, 80 percent of all pants sold are jeans. In 1970, stores there sold 1.2 million suits and 3.5 million pairs of jeans. Two decades later, the same stores were selling half as many suits and three times as much denim. In Amsterdam, 40 percent of the population wears a pair of jeans on any given day. Levi Strauss & Co. now sells its designs in more than 100 countries around the world. Looking for a pair of Lee's? You can pick them up in department stores in Australia, Austria, Belgium, Canada, France, Germany, Greece, Hungary, Iceland, Ireland, Israel, Italy, Poland, Portugal, Spain, Sweden, Switzerland, Turkey, or the United Kingdom. They're not just in Kansas any more.

Jeans have survived countless transformations, from work pants to army gear to play clothes and, eventually, school clothes. But they've never been such an accepted part of our wardrobe as they are today. We wear them practically everywhere, pulling on a pair for school or for a lazy Saturday afternoon hanging out with friends. People wear them to work in casual offices, or to formal offices on Fridays. The kids in the arcade, the skateboarders outside, and the people driving by are all wearing them. Some churches even encourage their members to wear jeans, as a way of including people of every background and status level. Just as school uniforms make all students appear equal, jeans make all people appear equal. You can't tell the difference between a farmer and a politician when they're both wearing jeans.

At the same time, the subtle differences in our jeans reveal something about our personalities. Someone wearing the latest designer label is saying, "I keep up with fashion, I can afford the best, and appearances are important to me." The guy wearing a pair salvaged from the Salvation Army might be hinting, "I can be cool without spending tons of money."

Whatever our pants are saying about us, there's no doubt that we love our jeans. The average American owns seven pairs, and Canadians have almost as many. Why? Because jeans are sexy (you can wear them on a date) but casual (you won't look like you're trying too hard). They're stylish (you'll look like a

magazine ad) but comfortable (you can still eat dinner).

Jeans act as the perfect backdrop, the same way white walls in a gallery make the art stand out better. With a safe base of denim, we can try out a baby T or a bright halter top, or slip on a shaggy sweater. After more than 100 years, jeans continue to gain popularity because, for many of us, a new pair is like a blank canvas waiting for the imprint of our own personality.

Even in the 1930s and 1940s, jeans ads were everywhere. There were billboards at rodeos, photos in magazines, and even giant pairs of jeans hanging from telephone poles.

SOURCES

Introduction

American History: Lee Jeans 101.
Merriam, KS: The Lee Company, 2000.

"Blue Jean Workout." *Outside*, September 2004, p. 30.

Douillard, André, and Jean-Marc St-Pierre, producers. *How It's Made* [video]. Carson City, NV: Filmwest Associates, 2001.

Goode, Stephen. "Blue-Jean Power." *Insight on the News*, August 16, 1999.

Le Couteur, Penny, and Jay Burreson. *Napoleon's Buttons*. New York: Penguin Putnam, 2003.

Yates, D.A., and G. Jones. "Casual Dress Days: Are there bottom-line impacts?" *Organization Development Journal*, 1998, pp. 107–11.

Chapter 1: The Birth of the Blues

"About LS & Co." From the website of Levi Strauss & Co. (www.levistrauss.com/about).

"About the Gold Rush." From the website of PBS (www.pbs.org/goldrush/allabout.html).

Adkins, Jan. "The Evolution of Jeans." *Mother Earth News*, July–August 1990, p. 60.

Legan, Gary, producer. *The History of Blue Jeans* [video]. West Long Branch, NJ: Estate Films, 1995.

"San Francisco Facilities in the Early 1950s." From the website of the Virtual Museum of the City of San Francisco (www.sfmuseum.org/hist/56facts.html).

Chapter 2: Movers and Shakers and Blue Jean Makers

George-Warren, Holly, and Michelle Freedman. *How the West Was Worn*. New York: Harry N. Abrams, 2001.

Gromer, Cliff. "Levi's Jeans." *Popular Mechanics*, May 1999, p. 94.

"Our History." From the website of Lee Jeans (www.leejeans.com/about_leejeans_history.asp).

Patoski, Joe Nick. "True Fit." *Texas Monthly*, September 1993, p. 120.

Rodengen, Jeffrey L. *The Legend of VF Corporation*. Fort Lauderdale, FL: Write Stuff Enterprises, 1998.

Chapter 3: Blue Jean Time Machine

Harris, Carol. "Women Under Fire in World War II." From the website of the BBC (www.bbc.co.uk/history/war/wwtwo/women_at_war_03.shtml).

"The Teenagers." *Newsweek*, March 21, 1966.

Chapter 4: The Jean Scene

Barker, Olivia. "Nothing comes between teens and their jeans—not even..." *USA Today*, September 5, 2002.

Barol, B., and E.A. Leonard. "Anatomy of a Fad." *Newsweek*, Summer/Fall 1990, p. 40.

Browne, Malcolm W. "Yugoslavs Foil Jeans Bootleggers." *New York Times*, March 20, 1977.

"The Esquire Guide: Denim." *Esquire*, June 2001, p. 77.

"History." From the website of Mavi Jeans (www.mavi.com/usa/).

Lentz, Ellen. "East Germans Line Up to Buy a Pair of Levi's." *New York Times*, November 30, 1978.

Lubove, S., and G. Slutsker. "Enzyme-Eaten Jeans." *Forbes*, October 29, 1990, p. 140.

Philips, Alan. "$300 for black-market jeans in Russia." *Globe and Mail*, December 3, 1979.

Chapter 5: Borderless Blues

"Blue Jeans: Bacteria." *Science World*, August 2, 2003, p. 10.

"Cotton." From the website of Microsoft Encarta Online Encyclopedia 2004 (encarta.msn.com/encyclopedia_761562256/Cotton.html).

Cox, Sarah. "Guess? what: Guess! Inc in Los Angeles are trendsetters in more ways than one (Sewing sweatshops make their products)." *New Internationalist*, June 1998, p. 25.

Herbert, Bob. "In America: A Sweatshop Victory." *New York Times*, December 22, 1995.

Jeffcott, Bob, and Lynda Yanz. "Bridging the GAP." *Our Times*, February 1997, p. 24.

Myers, Dorothy. "Cotton Tales." *New Internationalist*, May 2000, p. 24.

Nifong, Christina. "Raid Reveals Seamy Side of U.S. Garment-Making." *Christian Science Monitor*, August 16, 1995.

"NY ICE Breaks Massive $400M IPR Smuggling Group." *Inside ICE*, May 25–June 7, 2004, p. 4.

Schoenberger, Karl. *Levi's Children*. New York: Atlantic Monthly Press, 2000.

"The Shame of Sweatshops." *Consumer Reports*, August 1999, p. 18.

"Sweating for Fashion." *Economist*, March 6, 2004, p. 14.

"The World's Greatest Fakes." From the website of CBS News (www.cbsnews.com/stories/2004/01/26/60minutes).

Chapter 6: Panting for Perfection

Associated Press. "Clothes Made in Berlin Jail a Fashion Hit." October 9, 2003. From the website of the *Miami Herald* (http://www.miami.com/mld/miamiherald/6968492.htm?1c).

Bunn, Austin. "Not Fade Away." *New York Times Magazine*, December 1, 2002, p. 60.

"Jeans—the facts." *New Internationalist*, June 1998, p. 18.

Scott, Sarah. "Inside Avril's Pants." *National Post Business*, September 2003, p. 52.

INDEX

ACKNOWLEDGMENTS

The author gratefully acknowledges the assistance of Lynn Downey at Levi Strauss & Co. and Jennifer Johnson at Lee Jeans in researching the history of their companies. Downey and Johnson also provided invaluable help in researching and gathering together photographs for this book, as did Susan Downer at Wrangler, Tullia Marcolongo at the Maquila Solidarity Network, Lara Kimber at the Sciencenter, and Vyara Ndejuru at Parasuco Jeans. Laura Carter and Neil Kearney at the International Textile, Garment and Leather Workers' Federation provided helpful information on the garment industry and ethical shopping. The quote on page 6 is excerpted from *The Sisterhood of the Traveling Pants* by Ann Brashares. It is used with the permission of Random House, Inc.

PHOTO CREDITS

ABOUT THE AUTHOR

Tanya Lloyd Kyi finished writing *The Blue Jean Book* when she was nine months pregnant. She could only stare at her favorite pair of Gap jeans and hope that one day they would fit again. When she's not delving into the world of pop culture, Tanya spends her time running, reading, and writing. She is the author of *True Stories from the Edge: Fires!, My Time as Caz Hazard, Truth,* and *Canadian Girls Who Rocked the World.*

She lives in Vancouver with her husband Min and daughter Julia.